Last Chance in Europe

Books by Charles O. Lerche, Jr.

Principles of International Politics

Foreign Policy of the American People

Readings in International Politics

Concepts of International Politics (*with A. A. Said*)

America in World Affairs

The Uncertain South

The Cold War . . . and After

Last Chance in Europe

LAST CHANCE IN EUROPE. Bases for a New American Policy
by Charles O. Lerche, Jr.

Foreword by Kenneth W. Thompson

CHICAGO QUADRANGLE BOOKS 1967

Library of Congress Catalog Card Number: 67-12351

To MARGARET and HERKY

Foreword

Charles O. Lerche was a restless mind unsparing of himself, his friends, or his subjects as he pursued the search for truth. *Last Chance in Europe* is his eighth book. He contributed more major studies in his all too brief career than most scholars complete in a long lifetime. His texts have become standard fare for students of international politics. No one can claim more success in challenging readers to break free from the shackles of a merely descriptive and factual approach to world problems. It will come as no surprise to those who know his work that he calls in *Last Chance* for "a new set of assumptions, a new orienting concept . . ." The richest legacy of his writings is a coherently worked out collection of principles and workable concepts. He gave us tools and methods of analysis no less than thoughtful and challenging interpretations of foreign and domestic policies.

The foundations of Lerche's approach to the problems of Europe are faithful to his earlier writings. He invites a clearer formulation by American policy-makers of our national interest with an accompanying clarity on priorities and goals. If we find the Marxist division of the world into communist and non-communist states too simple, why are we satisfied with a global separation of peoples into communist and anti-communist? Lerche believes there is a far wider spectrum of political doctrines and economic systems. We must learn to live with variety not because we approve in every case but because our national interest requires it.

Last Chance is the work of a deeply troubled scholar and teacher who witnessed first-hand the deterioration of the friendly relations Americans enjoyed with Europe in the era of the Marshall Plan. In seeking the causes for this decline, Lerche analyzes the differing assumptions Europeans and Americans bring to the contemporary crisis. Architects of recent American policy may find him severe. It may be that rigidities Lerche discovers in their outlook partly disappear if their private, as distinct from public, views are explored. Yet Lerche deals not with individuals or personal failures. His subject is the dominant underlying theme of the American outlook. Even those who would be less outspoken in appraising American policy toward Europe will recognize the symptoms Lerche describes. For who can deny the impulsiveness of our crusade to save Europe, which we all too often attribute to lofty aims and unselfishness, but which Europeans see as a practical response to political realities? Or who has not witnessed the struggle between Europe-firsters and Asia-firsters and the ebb and flow of prevailing influence by one and the other trend of thought? Is there any doubt that our self-righteousness has seemed insufferable to Europeans whose postwar weakness could not obscure their historic greatness? And is there any doubt that the "Cold War" has had a less militant emphasis in Europe at least in recent months?

Yet whatever differences the student of world affairs may bring to the reading of *Last Chance,* those who struggle to make sense of international problems will forever be in Charles Lerche's debt. For his timeless contribution in this as in earlier writings is through fervor and logic to force us to pay heed to what might otherwise suffer neglect. Not only the eyes of American policy-makers but of the public at large have focused almost exclusively on Vietnam. Professor Lerche's powerful study brings us back to the lasting importance of America's relations with Europe. His words and evidence drawn from history and personal experience will, in the years ahead, stir and inspire Americans to recall that on both moral and political grounds, our destiny has been and remains intertwined with Europe. And in periods of neglect, such as Lerche considers we are experiencing today, those who shape policy will have to answer to this outspoken but always compassionate critic.

Thus while Charles Lerche has written his last book, his philosophy lives on. Because his subjects are fundamental, his wisdom endures. It would be wrong to pretend that had he lived he would not have revised certain views or changed his mind on specific policy questions. What is important is the fact that he, by comparison with many essayists or reporters of the flow of events, had a framework for viewing problems. Others in their day may examine and appraise his approach, using it in whole or in part or dismissing it. He had a sense of proportion and reality and this may be imitated. Above all, there was a passion for searching out the real issues, the most stubborn problems of the day. If students and scholars possessed by the need to play it safe or fascinated exclusively by theoretical niceties and abstractions seek renewal, they could do worse than to review the works of "a scholar and gentleman," Charles O. Lerche.

KENNETH W. THOMPSON
The Rockefeller Foundation

Preface

In the past few years a literal flood of books has dealt with the rapid changes in American relations with Western Europe since the end of World War II. Candor and a decent respect for my readers, therefore, prompt me to spell out my rationale for writing this book.

This book rests upon my lifetime professional concern with American foreign policy and upon a fairly extensive acquaintance with contemporary Western Europe. During the past eight years I have made seven trips to Europe, all involving more than one country and ranging in duration from one to nine months. My roles in Europe have been varied: visiting professor at two academic institutions, research scholar, an "American Specialist" with the Department of State on two occasions, adviser to a task force of congressmen, and plain and simple tourist.

In the course of these visits I have expounded upon, discussed, argued over, and lectured about European-American relations before audiences of all sizes and in small informal groups. In the process I have become acquainted with what might be called "European opinion" from my contacts with political, academic, business, and opinion leaders in Western Europe. Exchanging ideas with so many

Europeans in so many countries over a decade, I have become aware of a great and glaring fact: the assumptions about Europe on which the United States has proceeded since 1945, and on which it operates today, are seriously out of phase with contemporary reality. European-American relations are in major crisis today, but the difficulties have their roots in the image of Europe that Americans developed and accepted immediately after World War II, and to which they have remained faithful ever since. If we are to stop the downward slide of Atlantic relations and restore them to something like stability and warmth, the U.S. image of the problem must undergo a major overhaul and modernization.

This book, therefore, has a dual theme. Its first purpose is to present in general terms the reality of the European political scene, especially in contrast to the euphoric portrait which Washington has accepted for so long. Second, it suggests the outline of a new set of assumptions, a new orienting concept, and a new policy that I believe are more realistic and more hopeful of productive result.

No technical discussions of military doctrine, economic theory, or constitutional practice will be found in the pages that follow. Charles de Gaulle is correct on at least one basic point: political decisions on matters of purpose and principle are the *sine qua non* of any improvement in European-American relations; tinkering with committees and task forces will never solve basic political problems. This book therefore attempts to establish the terms of the fundamental political confrontation in Europe today and the basic decisions that the American people must make in the (fairly near) future. America is rapidly approaching its "last chance in Europe"; failure to seize the opportunity will have portentous and long-lasting consequences.

I gratefully acknowledge the confidence and faith of many friends and colleagues in both Europe and the United

States who have urged me to complete this book. Now that I have done so, I can only hope that they do not have cause to regret their insistence. William F. Ahlstrom, of American University, not only edited the manuscript with rare consistency but also was a source of data and inspiration. My wife, Margaret Evans Lerche, was as always a source of encouragement and stimulus throughout the preparation of this book; her lack of agreement with some parts of the argument never prevented her from assisting me in every way possible with the laborious process of creation.

For all errors of fact and miscalculations of judgment, of course, I assume full responsibility.

C. O. L.

Washington, D.C., 1966

Contents

Last Chance in Europe

Chapter One
The Premise:
Western Europe
and American
Foreign Policy

From Europe the first immigrants came to the New World. Against Europe the young United States rebelled in the eighteenth century. In defiance of Europe Americans preached the doctrine of "isolationism" during the nineteenth century. To Europe Americans returned in force in 1917 and 1944. In Europe the initial encounters of the Cold War took place. And, finally, in Europe the United States has made its most binding, inclusive, and long-lasting foreign commitments since 1945. From its very beginning as a nation, the United States has found its history and its destiny closely intertwined with the states and peoples of Western Europe.

Since the end of World War II the entire course of American foreign policy has been shaped to a great extent by Western Europe and its problems. Although the theory and the policy of containment—the skeleton of all U.S. thought and action for the past two decades—was originally cast in a global framework (calling as it did for a restraining ring of American-supported power around the Soviet heartland), in practice the European sector from 1947 onward was considered the most important one. The experience the United States gained in the early days of the struggle with communism in Europe has colored the foreign-policy attitudes of an entire generation of Americans. It is to this phenomenon and to this generation that most of what follows in this book is directed.

The Original American Commitment to Europe

The Cold War, and with it the major components of postwar American foreign policy, began in Europe. It is necessary and useful to review briefly the major reasons why the United States made its first overt anti-communist moves there. Looking back on the immediate postwar period is difficult—and frequently unpleasant—for middle-aged Americans, while younger ones need to be reminded again and again of the decisions that have led directly to the nation's contemporary predicament. Why, then, did the United States choose to take its stand in Central and Western Europe?

In general terms, two reasons may be suggested: importance and criticality. In 1946 and 1947 Europe was the region most vulnerable to Soviet pressure and at the same time the most valuable prize within Moscow's reach. The Soviet Union, if its thrust for world domination was to be stopped at all, first had to be stopped in Europe. Failure there would mean ultimate failure everywhere.

The Soviet threat to Europe was twofold. On the one

hand, Moscow menaced the continent with its Red Army, kept almost intact after the war while the Western Allies systematically demobilized their forces. Soviet troops were deployed all along the newly created (and newly named) Iron Curtain. On the other hand, in several of the unstable democracies of the West, internal communist takeover was a real danger, especially in the two major states where the Communist party had achieved mass proportions, France and Italy. Thus, from the very beginning of the struggle, the United States saw itself fighting a simultaneous battle against communist influence on two fronts, internal and external. This preoccupation rapidly became a fixed concern in all American policy. Everywhere in the world today, Americans perceive twin facets of the communist threat: internal subversion and external aggression.

Europe was not only the most exposed sector of the non-communist world in the late 1940's; it was also the one the United States felt it could least afford to lose. Although shattered by war and divided by the Iron Curtain, apparently incapable of either economic recovery or political stability, Europe's potential was so great that at all costs it had to be held for the West. The Soviet Union's power obviously would be comparable—once the devastation of the war had been repaired—to that of the United States. Were Moscow to gain Europe's power, the balance would be tipped permanently and disastrously against the United States. But European and American power combined would far outweigh even the greatest Soviet effort.

This original American strategy was aimed not only at denying the European states to Soviet aggression but also at preserving Europe's power for the American camp. Containment was, after all, a global concept, and for the United States to attempt—under 1947 conditions—to hold the enormous line alone was impossible (as it still is under the conditions of the 1960's). A recovered Europe, protected from Soviet assault and with its internal problems solved with American assistance, would be able to add great increments of military, political, and economic power to the free world's strategy for checkmating Soviet aggression. As early as the initiation of the Marshall Plan, it was obvious that Washington had extensive designs for the European states it was hurrying to succor.

The details of American policy in and toward Europe have changed considerably since the end of the war, but general outlines have remained substantially intact. Between 1947 and 1951 the United States set itself three major tasks in Europe that later became universalized and pursued everywhere in the world. They were (and are): first, to bring about European economic recovery and political stability; second, to place Europe under the protection of the American strategic nuclear umbrella by means of a credible guarantee; third, to organize Europe for its own defense and for the extension of its power into extra-European areas under American leadership and with close American cooperation.

The first of these tasks was attacked by means of the Marshall Plan, the second by the North Atlantic Treaty, and the third by the creation of the organizational apparatus of NATO. Great and unexpectedly rapid success greeted the early implementation of each of these missions —so much success, indeed, that many of the contemporary traumas of America's European policy are traceable to the quick and almost effortless victories the United States won in Europe in the early years of the Cold War. At home, American policy-makers came to expect inevitable and permanent primacy.

The Rise of the "Anti-Europeans"

The focus on Europe that marked the early years of the Cold War, however, was never unanimously accepted in the United States. Responding to an urge well over a century old, many earnest citizens during the late 1940's felt that Europe offered only entanglement and frustration, that the true destiny of the United States was to be found in Latin America and especially in the Far East. A traditional American anti-European bias has provided something of an *obbligato* to the main theme of United States policy throughout the Cold War.

Throughout the nineteenth century and up to World War I, American foreign policy was built on two principal elements. The first was American independence of European affairs and involvements; the second was a sphere of relatively unchallenged American influence in Latin America and Asia. The Monroe Doctrine and the Open Door, although separated in time by more than seventy-five years, were cut from the same ideological pattern: "isolationism" in Europe, activist intervention in other areas. The interwar period after 1920 showed the same trends, as isolationist Republican administrations nevertheless involved the United States in both Latin America (although this was eventually softened by the "Good Neighbor" approach) and in the Far East (via the Nine-Power Treaty, the "Stimson Doctrine," and the quarrels with Japan that eventually led to Pearl Harbor).

By the time World War II came to America, the lines were drawn sharply. The prewar isolationists and non-interventionists became "Asia-firsters" during the war; they complained throughout the conflict that General MacArthur's Pacific front was being systematically starved to feed General Marshall's (and General Eisenhower's) European war. The interventionists of 1940, on the other hand, became generally the "Europe-firsters" of 1942, subscribing wholeheartedly to President Roosevelt's strategy of crushing Germany before turning full American strength against Japan. The split was not confined to the general public but also found expression at the highest levels of government. The Department of State, for example, was sharply divided into three mutually hostile, suspicious, and competitive camps of specialists in (and often apologists for) Latin America, the Far East, and Europe.

Thus, the American decision to move first in Europe as the Cold War began, whatever else it might have been, was a victory for the Europe-first groups in and out of government. The very vigor and speed of United States moves in Europe only served to inspire the anti-Europe groups to greater pressures; they hoped to recall the United States to the correct and only profitable path—the non-European parts of the American political world. It was not long before the Far Eastern group discovered its opportunity; Latin America's turn was not to come for more than a decade.

As early as 1948 voices began to plead for "saving" China from imminent conquest by communism. In part there were political reasons. The Marshall Plan had been passed by the Republican 80th Congress and had therefore been wrapped in the mantle of bipartisanship. But Thomas E. Dewey discovered early in his presidential campaign that bipartisanship had never been overtly extended to China, and he made what capital he could out of Far Eastern affairs (which, as it turned out, was not very much). His attempt, however, did revive the pro-Asia camp, and the subsequent collapse of China provided an issue around which its members could rally.

The Korean War, of course, brought the Asia-firsters

back to stage center. Not only did Korea prove—to them at least—the centrality of Asia to American foreign concerns; it also provided a valuable outlet for the frustrated militancy of the anti-communist crusade. For all its heady rhetoric, the Cold War in Europe provided discouragingly few emotional releases, and public pressure for "action" was growing to the point of danger. In Korea there were real communists, not only to hate but also to shoot at. Thus, the Asia-firsters, aided by the McCarthy hysteria, could and did argue that "their" part of the world was not only the most important but also the most interesting and psychically satisfying.

The Decline of European Issues

From 1953 virtually to the present, two related trends in American policy have been moving steadily in opposite directions. On the one hand, crises in Asia (and more recently in Latin America and Africa) have been growing in frequency; on the other, European-American relations (at least as viewed from the United States) have assumed an increasingly institutionalized and formalized pattern, with a corresponding decline in official and popular interest. Crisis in Asia, Africa, or Latin America tends to involve subversion, revolution, ideological dispute, military threats, and even open war. But crisis in Europe (except for occasional flare-ups over Berlin) tends to be rather boring, involving dreary questions of economics or defense strategy.

Furthermore, there is the myth of American success. This point will be discussed in detail in later chapters; here its role can be seen as support for the argument that the U.S. record of success in Europe means fewer decisions and fewer worries, while in Asia the American position, never very strong, is weakening daily. The difficulties bred by success are apparently considered less serious than those stemming from failure.

Another element in the decline in the relative importance of European issues has been the gradual but steady replacement of the Soviet Union by China as America's principal enemy. Analysts of Soviet phenomena tend to approach their subject from a European point of view (a surprising number of the "Kremlinologists" now operating in the United States are of Central or Eastern European birth), while the latter-day Sinologists being produced in the United States today tend to view China in a Far Eastern, an Asian, or a non-Western context. The evolution of Soviet-American relations from conflict through détente to parallelism has, as a by-product, strengthened China's position as the leading adversary of United States policies. The operative conclusion to be drawn from the Sino-Soviet split is self-evident: Russia declines as the major threat in Europe; China, the major threat to Asia, grows daily in menace. The controlling demands on American policy, therefore, flow from Asia.

All these lines converge in the most acute crisis area of the mid-1960's: Southeast Asia. We shall deal only indirectly with this troubled region, but clearly one significant result of American preoccupation with Southeast Asia has been a further downgrading of Europe and its problems. This can be seen at two levels.

In the first place, the American adventure in Southeast Asia has placed serious strains upon relations with a number of European states. Some, like West Germany, object to American policy because they feel that Washington is neglecting its major interests to pursue a secondary mission at the opposite end of the world. Others, like France, feel that American policy in Southeast Asia is risky, unwise, and ultimately unsuccessful, and refuse to be identified with it. In either case the result is the same: a further weakening of the Atlantic alliance.

The second consequence of the Southeast Asian crisis is the emergence of a generally perfunctory American approach to the problems of contemporary Europe, featuring well worn clichés and much perfervid oratory, but few solid initiatives. Taking shelter behind traditional—but politically obtuse—arguments that "the war comes first," the United States since 1961 has sought to meet its European concerns in a mood of almost absent-minded preoccupation.

Tricky proposals like the Multi-Lateral Nuclear Force (MLF), obviously built on the premise that large numbers of Europeans are stupid enough to take illusion for reality (in the form of a "sense of participation" in nuclear decisions over which the United States retains full veto power), have only pointed up American unwillingness to grapple with the complex reality of today's Europe. The rhetoric of fear, with which American policy-makers have long sought to frighten Europeans into loyalty to American leadership, is threadbare; Europeans, watching the United States move ponderously and painfully in the direction of a new Soviet-American relationship, no longer feel any pressing need to rally behind the United States to repel the invader at the gate. Instead, Europeans ask today in all sincerity: "Is the United States really interested in us any more?"

The Basic Question of Priorities

What is really involved here is the old—but never resolved —question of priorities of American foreign policy. The United States, as Senator J. William Fulbright has so cogently pointed out as to earn for himself a considerable

measure of calumny,* cannot do everything. It must apportion its limited (though enormous) capabilities among
major matters of continuing interest, leaving lesser problems to be handled with only minor commitments of
American power, or with no commitments at all. This approach seems neither obscure nor complex, yet U.S. policy-
makers have not been able to apply it throughout the entire
postwar period.

The reason for this failure—and failure it is—is not hard
to find. Priorities are judgments about relative importance
and can only be established in terms of an overriding national purpose. The "importance" of any particular enterprise is the measure of its relevance to this national purpose.
If there is agreement on even highly generalized ideas of
mission, the allocation of priorities to various concerns becomes feasible—although often painful. When there is no
general purpose for national policy, priorities cannot be
established.

This is not the place for a detailed discussion of the confusion of purpose in American foreign policy, although it is
obviously one of the central issues that must be faced. This
much, however, must be said: at the operational level, in
concrete situations demanding decision and action, the
United States has far too often resorted to "policy by reaction." Instead of determining what it ought to be doing in
a particular situation, Washington has taken the easy way
by first determining what the Kremlin was seeking and
then attempting to frustrate those communist objectives.
Instead of establishing their own clear goals and devising a
policy to achieve them, American policy-makers have
merely tried to defeat whatever communist policies might
be operating in the immediate context.

This working definition of American purpose—to op-

* See his *Old Myths and New Realities* (New York, 1964), especially
Chapter 1.

pose communist initiatives everywhere and at all times—
has had a clear and predictable effect on American priority
judgments. For all practical purposes, Washington has permitted communist doctrine and behavior to determine what
is important to the United States. Wherever the communists
may move, there the United States must also immediately
move; conversely, any area in which the communist danger
does not exist, is quiescent, or has been beaten back, is less
important than an active theater.

Still concentrating on operational considerations, a second priority-inducing element can be identified: contempo-
raneity. Today's crisis—whatever it may be—is assumed by
the American government, the press, and most of the public
to be the most important issue facing the nation. Yesterday's
problem is history, and tomorrow's cannot yet be dealt with
(anticipating difficulties demands answering "hypothetical
questions," something the foreign-policy Establishment of
the United States stubbornly refuses to do). So the simple
march of history also imposes its own stern but ever-chang-
ing priority on American decision-making.

This is the present framework of European-American
relations, at least as viewed from Washington. When the
Soviet threat to Europe was immediate and massive, the
United States gave top priority to the region; as the threat
has receded relatively and absolutely, and as other areas
have come under communist attack, Europe's share of
American attention and resources has declined. Europe
has had its turn, and now it must balance its accounts.
Rather than continuing to press their own parochial and
often selfish interests upon the United States, the honorable
course for Europeans today would be to join their new
strength with America's in meeting the new generation of
threats to the commonweal.

However clear and self-evident this theory may seem on
the banks of the Potomac, it simply never has been ac-

cepted on the banks of the Seine, the Rhine, the Tiber, or even the Thames. When Europeans wonder today if the United States is interested in them any longer, they are really asking whether Europe in its own right has any standing in American eyes—or must it be reconciled to being judged in terms of its role, as defined by Washington, in a global (that is, extra-European) struggle with communism?

We argue an entirely different point of view. It is based on the premise that priority judgments in American foreign policy are far more than functions of the ebb and flow of the Cold War, that instead they should be made within the context of the best long-range interests of the nation. On that basis, therefore, we advance the thesis that European-American relations have been, are today, and will indefinitely remain the most important single dimension of American foreign policy. If the network of contacts between Western Europe and the United States is strained and ineffective, and if—as is the case today—a steadily widening gulf has already opened, "victories" in other parts of the world cannot balance the weakness of this key element in American policy.

In one sense, this argument is a return to the original principles that motivated American decisions between 1947 and 1949. Underlying all the "realism" and power-political implications of the Marshall Plan and the North Atlantic Treaty was a poorly verbalized but powerful feeling in the United States that Europe and America belonged together.

A viable and permanent partnership dedicated to common concerns—with inevitable disagreements confined to quiet resolution—in a context much broader than the contemporary Cold War would seem not only a desirable but also an attainable goal. If, in the process of readjusting its thinking and its policies vis-à-vis Western Europe, the United States finds itself obliged to discard some of its cherished shibboleths, and to modify some of its postures in non-European regions of the world, who is to say now that the nation will be the loser? The United States saved Europe between 1946 and 1951; in the 1960's and 1970's Western Europe may well have an opportunity to return the compliment.

Chapter Two
The Image:
How Americans
See Europe

The past two decades have been difficult years for Americans as they have sought to find a path through the tangled and bewildering thickets of world affairs. Thrust into a role of world leadership before they were emotionally prepared, called upon to respond effectively to an unending series of crises, the American people have never had time since 1945 fully to recover their balance and take stock coolly of their goals, their resources, and their policies. Forced to extemporize a *Weltanschauung* almost overnight in the aftermath of World War II, Americans made a valiant effort to develop working hypotheses explaining their predicament and pointing the way to final vindication and success. These have become the foundations of American action.

The very speed of U.S. moves in many parts of the world has unfortunately invalidated many of the early assumptions upon which American policy was based. The list of postulates that have been cruelly used by the history of the past twenty years is long, but even a brief catalog suggests the rude shocks to which Americans have been subjected. The permanence of the wartime alliance, the effectiveness of the United Nations, the nuclear monopoly of the United States, the ubiquity of the bipolar Cold War, and the inevitable friendliness of the emerging nations are only a few of the cherished illusions of American policy that have proved ephemeral. No wonder so many Americans in the 1960's see themselves wandering in a strange universe fraught with danger and with almost no guideposts.

Throughout the vicissitudes of the era of the Cold War and until very recently, however, one fixed point in the U.S. policy universe has comforted and reassured Americans in times of trouble. No matter how unstable any other part of the world might seem, or how ambiguous and difficult the American road, Washington and the public alike have felt they could count on loyal and effective support from America's allies in Western Europe. The initial moves of the United States into the Old World in 1947 and 1948 provoked a flood of rhetoric and a deluge of highly emotionalized pledges of eternal fealty; once committed, Americans have never looked back. Western Europe and its daughter, the United States, had finally healed the breach of 1776 and together faced a hostile world.

In all their approaches to Western Europe since 1947, Americans have been motivated by a consciousness of common destiny and shared responsibilities that does great credit to the nation's idealism. Americans believed in 1948 that they had the historic and moral duty to "save" Europe; they believe the same thing today. When Europeans interpret contemporary U.S. policy in a pejorative way, Americans simply do not understand. Why should the nation's generous and self-sacrificing policies be dismissed as attempts to perpetuate American "hegemony" over its European allies?

Why should its noble concept of an "Atlantic community" based on "interdependence" be received critically and coolly in Western Europe as a scheme of "domination"? It baffles Americans that Europeans today seem to show so little gratitude for past sacrifices, so little appreciation of present efforts. What, the people ask, is wrong with Europeans; why can't they understand—and be moved by—the obvious good intentions of the United States?

Although there are many answers to this question, some of which will be suggested below, the central problem can be simply stated: maladjustments in European-American relations today flow primarily from that ancient dilemma of human relations, the disparity between image and reality. Affected by history and the political imperatives of the moment, the United States constructed an image of postwar Europe that suited the requirements of the environment (at home and abroad) of the late 1940's. Fortunately for all concerned, this image was sufficiently akin to reality to allow a viable relationship. But in the years since, Europe has become a drastically different phenomenon than it was in 1946 or 1950, while the American image of Europe, on which Washington still bases its most important decisions, has not been updated.

Thus, the United States persists today in talking to (or at least appearing to talk to) the Europe of 1949, while Europe lives in the 1960's and is quite obviously looking forward to the 1970's and beyond. No wonder transatlantic discussions tend so often to bog down in mutual incomprehensibility or else to drift into empty but heated recriminations. Tension and incipient crisis in European-American relations are not entirely due to the stubbornness or obtuseness of European leaders (although this plays a role); to a large extent they have their origin in the peculiar interpretations of North Atlantic ties advanced by Americans.

Since there is little the United States can do to change

the way Europe looks at itself and the rest of the world, it seems self-evident that the beginning of a more healthy relationship lies in analyzing the controlling American image of Europe, determining where it falls significantly short of reality, and at least speculating on what changes might be made. Foreign policy always begins with identification of a problem. In no area of American foreign policy is there greater need for improvement in problem identification than in that of Western Europe.

The Traditional American Approach to Europe

The prevailing American attitude toward Europe—at least in a political sense—is rooted in ambivalence. On the one hand, the close and continuous link between the cultures, the economies, and the political systems of North America and Western Europe, first established during the colonial period and unimpaired to the present, binds the United States intimately to Europe's destiny. On the other hand, however, there is the stubborn historical fact—so central to the self-image of the United States—that the birth of the United States was brought about by forcible separation from the European motherland, and that American independence, resisted by Britain, was achieved only after a successful war. Thus, America has always acknowledged being a child of Europe but has consistently rebelled against its parentage; it has been tied to the "old country" by blood and tradition, but it has been politically hostile to and suspicious of the machinations and wiles of European governments.

From the first decade of independence until the very eve of Pearl Harbor, Americans have argued that they are a special people, committed to a loftier mission than ordinary states and conducting a policy more high-minded, more disinterested, and more humane. This was the basis of what Americans for so long incorrectly called "isolationism." It was not a question of refusing to deal with other states in the international order, but rather a refusal to deal with them except on American terms. No assumption about the role of the United States in the world has been more tenacious than the insistence that Americans were *in* the world political system but emphatically were not *of* it. For the whole of American history, U.S. statesmen have sought the ears of the rest of the world to proclaim the nation as the fountainhead of new ideas and actions for the reordering of international relationships. Yet now, when American power and status have conferred that attention upon the United States, it seems powerless to offer other than shopworn clichés and pat formulas, especially about European-American relationships. Instead of a new and vigorous dynamic for North Atlantic relations, Washington seems content with the rituals of twenty years ago, intoxicated by the early successes that they engendered, oblivious to the fact that they no longer fit present realities.

Washington's Farewell Address asked: "Why quit our own to stand on foreign ground?" and answered by pointing out that "our detached and distant position invites us and enables us to pursue a different course" from the states of Europe. Jefferson's Inaugural Address summed up American aspirations toward Europe in the famous formula of "peace, friendship, and trade with all nations; entangling alliances with none." The Monroe Doctrine foreswore any American interest, present or future, in "the wars of the European powers," because "the political system of the allied powers is essentially different in this respect from that of America." In each subsequent decade of the nineteenth century and into the early years of the twentieth, equivalent, if less rhetorically effective, reinforcements of the same point were made by successive generations of American statesmen.

Behind this self-denying ordinance of American policy was the conviction that in Europe the United States could win no worthwhile prizes; instead, only deceit, disillusion, and humiliation awaited the unfortunate or unwise American statesman who permitted himself to be drawn into the European "cockpit." When Americans anathematized "power politics," they were thinking of Europe; "spheres of influence," "buffer states," "imperialism," and all the other entries in the lexicon of nineteenth-century international politics were indelibly branded with the clever but malign European genius.

The American attempt to transform international relations from a Europe-centered power-political system into an American-conceived rule of democracy and law was not the single-handed creation of Woodrow Wilson, although he receives most of the credit for it today. What contemporary Americans call "Wilsonianism" can be traced back to the early years of American history, when exuberant patriots foresaw the world-wide triumph of American political ideas and ideals, including, of course, American doctrines on peace, war, and international relations. Until World War I gave Wilson an opportunity to put his ideas into practice by means of mobilized American power, however, the hope of the United States lay in the putative power of example. American public figures expressed themselves unequivocally on the compelling force of their own conduct, but none more explicitly than Secretary of State William Seward in 1862: "The American people must be content to recommend the cause of human progress by the wisdom with which they should exercise the powers of self-government."

Besides this powerful ideological root there was a more practical reason underlying American isolation: Americans, to put it bluntly, were afraid of Europe. The world today is much more aware than it was in the nineteenth century of the "postcolonial mentality." Contemporary statesmen are highly sensitive to the mixture of resentment and dependence that characterizes the attitudes of a newly independent ex-colony toward its former rulers. Throughout the formative years of American diplomacy, the highly ideologized American condemnations of European duplicity only imperfectly concealed the other face of the problem. The United States was determined to stay out of European affairs (as well as keep Europe out of American concerns, *vide* the Monroe Doctrine), because Americans had serious doubts about their own ability to maintain and adequately advance their own interests in a European environment. Europeans were too clever and too experienced for Americans; safety lay only in non-involvement.

During the almost nine decades between independence and the end of the American Civil War, this acceptance of a peripheral role by the United States comported rather nicely with the facts of international life. The United States was weak, and the odds were that American entry into intra-European affairs would have been as disastrous as the prevailing orthodoxy contended. After 1865, however, this argument withered; Europe, watching American military capability as demonstrated in the Civil War, was perfectly willing to accept the United States as a full member of the system. But the United States would have none of it. No lack of physical competence was alleged as a pretext for isolation after Appomattox, but rather a tacit admission of the intellectual and moral incapability of Americans to cope with the chancelleries of the Old World.

At no time was this point made more clearly than in the aftermath of bitterness following World War I. The rejection of Wilson's peace package (that included not only the Covenant of the League of Nations but also, it should be remembered, the Treaty of Guarantee with France) was in the last analysis based on the fear that the United States would lose control over its own future and become only a

"pawn" of European politics. Wilson's attempt to transform Europe was abandoned as a failure, and the United
States spent the interwar years again hoping to convince
Europe of the folly of its ways by the sheer power of
example.

If Europe had the ability to cozen the United States almost at will, it followed that Europe could also competently
take care of its own affairs. It was literally inconceivable to
Americans that the center of world power and world politics
could not cope effectively with its own problems and the
tensions of its own region. American confidence in Europe's
political wisdom and capability was profound and persuasive, however deficient the United States might find European statesmen in political morality and high-mindedness.

The United States watched the coming of World War II
in this frame of mind. The rise of the dictators and the
deepening crisis in European affairs did little more than
confirm American judgments about the essentially evil nature of European politics. It seems never to have occurred
to U.S. leaders that Europe might not be able to control
itself, that they might be witnessing the death throes of
the order that had for so long been a fixed star in the world
political firmament. The outbreak of the war in 1939 produced a response in the United States that can only be
called smug: the agony of war was of course to be regretted,
but it was no more than Europe should have expected. As
for the United States, the policy line and the attitudes of the
general public agreed: *this* time, Americans would sit out
the whole affair.

The fall of France in 1940 broke the spell. Within a few
weeks, while the Nazi armies overran the continent and
turned toward a Britain seemingly destined to fall almost
without real resistance, the United States was forced to face
a series of grim facts. The most important was that Europe's
capacity to solve its own problems was exhausted. The

European system could no longer survive unaided, and the existence not only of unconquered Britain but of all free peoples depended upon the systematic application of American power to the European situation.

After a bitter debate at home, the United States poured itself unstintingly into the task of victory. The old fears of entrapment, deception, and defeat were laid aside "for the duration," and the wartime United Nations became the most effective fighting coalition in history. The United States, fighting the European phase of the war, saw itself in a real sense returning home to set things aright.

But old ideas die hard, and the lesson of World War II was at best incomplete. Americans came to appreciate during the war that Europe alone could no longer fight its wars to conclusions acceptable to the United States. Nevertheless, the idea persisted after V-E Day that in time of peace Europeans would prove equal to the tasks of reconstruction and postwar readjustment. Although pledged to remain in Europe after the war, and thus to avoid the error of hasty withdrawal, the United States still saw itself preparing for the day when it could cancel its commitment and leave Europe in the exclusive custody of Europeans.

The New American Image of Postwar Europe

Under this misapprehension, American sensibilities were shattered by Soviet intractability and the evolving Cold War. There was not only general dismay that the postwar peace had ended so soon and so abruptly; the real source of concern was that Americans found themselves facing a bitter and powerful enemy virtually alone. In the new drama of the Cold War, the Soviet Union had replaced Hitler's Germany as the major threat to world stability, while the United States was cast in the role played by Britain in 1940.

In 1946, however, there was a major difference. Behind
America after the war there stood no strong ally—as the
United States had stood behind Britain half a decade earlier
—which could be counted on to join the struggle and contribute to the ultimate victory. The United States stood at
the end of the line, and its defiance of Soviet aggression was
undertaken in an isolation that was splendid but exposed.
If the American people were to have any help in their conflict with communism, they had to discover and organize
useful allies.

The first place to turn for support and assistance, both
in logic and in view of the experience of the war, was to the
states of Western Europe. Here Americans hoped to find
strength where before they had discovered only weakness;
but here, instead of a number of governments each anxious
to contribute to a common cause, Americans encountered
a complex of crisis areas—the details differed but all shared
a common vulnerability to internal and external pressures.
Europe, historically the major generator and great ex-
porter of political power to the rest of the world, had become a "power vacuum" and the major target of extra-
European policy and power.

The rapid and disconcerting estimate of the situation in
Europe, which preceded initial American steps, was a genuinely traumatic experience for an entire generation of
American policy-makers. For State Department officials who
had matured in the shadow of the British Foreign Office, it
was a wrenching experience to realize that ultimate sanction and authority for world policy no longer rested in
Whitehall. For the American military community, the obliteration of the French and German armies from the
world's order of battle left a gap more conceptual than
operational, but exacerbating nonetheless. For dozens of
politicians, the absence of the comforting feeling that
nothing serious could happen to the United States in a

Europe-centered world was almost stupefying. For all Americans, the fact of European impotence was at least as great a shock as that of Soviet hostility.

But events refused to wait while the American people and their government came slowly and painfully to terms with this new environment. The crisis of the Cold War arose so rapidly that the necessary revolution in American attitudes was forced in a matter of only a few weeks during the spring of 1947. A revolution in outlook was indeed necessary, for Soviet threats, European weakness, and American determination to resist demanded a complete reversal of a policy more than 150 years old.

The history of American foreign policy from 1776 to 1941 taught one lesson: stay out of Europe. The war had brought about a minor modification in this principle: stay out of Europe except temporarily, and enter only to fight a major war against enemies that decent Europeans cannot handle by themselves. Now, facing neither peace nor war, the United States prepared to take on a massive commitment (of uncertain but probably extensive duration) in the maelstrom of European affairs. So complete a *volte-face,* against a policy supported by the prestige of the Founding Fathers, was possible only under conditions of major crisis abroad and great stress at home.

The eventual entry of the United States into Europe, via the Truman Doctrine, the Marshall Plan, and the North Atlantic Treaty, bore no evidence of the American struggle with its collective conscience. American policy during the late 1940's was bold, imaginative, and forceful— more so, indeed, than it has ever been since. Generally overlooked at the time, however, was the extent to which the American image of Europe had been changed as a necessary preliminary to mustering the nation's courage to risk its destiny in such troubled waters.

The nature of the new American attitude can be suggested in simple terms: once Americans became convinced that Europe was helpless on the brink of economic chaos, political collapse, and communist takeover, the fear of the Old World's superior political guile receded. No longer did the nation fear that its government, speaking through honest but unsophisticated leaders, would be led astray by Europe's clever diplomats. The popular mood changed dramatically with this realization. Instead of diffidence, the United States sought eagerly to demonstrate leadership; suspicion was replaced by trust, and self-doubt by an impressive self-confidence. The United States saw itself moving into the breach left by the collapse of the European system and, it must be admitted, rather enjoyed the spectacle.

Another way of putting the same point—albeit in somewhat more positive terms—is to suggest that the United States chose to emphasize its ancient cultural links with the motherland. Almost a "rediscovery" of Europe took place— at least in more or less sophisticated circles—between 1947 and 1949. Americans began to remind themselves of their European heritage, their nineteenth-century debt to the old European system that had enabled them to grow to maturity undisturbed by any major external crisis, and the common cause they had forged with Western Europe during two world wars. They gradually structured their mission as that of a strong and healthy child who returns to restore and preserve his aged parent, once powerful and prestigious but recently fallen on evil days.

What was wrong with Europe in 1947 that the United States felt called upon to right? What was the duty—in addition, of course, to the initial and pre-eminent one of stopping Soviet aggression—to which Americans were summoned? What changes in Europe's structure and dynamic did American policy-makers and the general public feel were necessary? Here the details of the changed American image of Europe in the postwar era can be seen somewhat more clearly.

In their analysis of Europe's problems, Americans used their own experience as a guide and their own country as a standard—a natural enough tendency that was to have unfortunate consequences in later years. What was fundamentally wrong with Europe, in other words, was that it was not the United States. The changes that Americans felt were necessary to save a battered Europe could be—and often were—identified as imports from America. In offering to share their substance, their insights, and their fate with Europeans, Americans were moved by a thoroughly sincere generosity. That Europeans were not quite as anxious to be saved by America as America was anxious to save Europeans was disregarded as untrue, irrelevant, or inevitably transitory.

The first and probably the most basic failing that the United States found in Europe was its disunity. With a population only slightly larger than that of the United States, non-communist Europe in 1947 was cut up into eighteen or nineteen distinct sovereignties, depending on whether or not Turkey was included in "Europe." To retain such anachronistically small units for organization, loyalty, and action seemed ridiculous to a United States aware of the enormous advantages it enjoyed from a single and highly centralized government.

Disunity was a highly practical difficulty. The United States had begun, even before the end of the war, extensive relief programs in the liberated countries and had extended the enterprise generally after the fighting stopped. Conducting such a large operation on the basis of a series of bilateral arrangements, one with each country affected, turned out to have two drawbacks. In the first place, it vastly complicated U.S. policy administration; in the second, it was an intrinsically wasteful and overlapping procedure which violated the ideals of mass production and distribution in which Americans placed such great faith.

From the very moment the United States first broached the Marshall Plan in June 1947, the disunity of Europe became a prime target of American action. Each subsequent step in American policy made the message more clear: Washington was determined to deal with "Europe" as a planning—and, so it was hoped, an operational—unit, and would do what it could to effect the concept. A few years later, when Europeans officially embraced the principle of "integration" and began to talk openly of eventual unity, Washington was overjoyed. At least one of the major efforts of American policy was bearing fruit.

A second major shortcoming of postwar Europe was its economic backwardness. In large part, Americans assumed this to be an unhappy heritage of the war, but they also felt that the real roots of the trouble lay much deeper than the destruction of industries or the confusion of corporate structures. In great measure, the economic stagnation of Europe three years after the end of the war was a function of its general disunity, as each little national economy sought to insulate itself from its fellows, to protect its domestic market, and to pursue more or less self-consciously the illusion of self-sufficiency. In fact, Europe's economic outlook even before the war was markedly different from that of the United States: American theory called for the production of floods of goods at the lowest possible prices, high turnover, low unit profit, and a relatively free market; Europeans, on the other hand, accepted cartels and combines, "restraint of trade," high unit profit, and relatively low turnover as the usual way to do business.

Americans, as they analyzed Europe's economic condition after the war, were convinced that their own mass-market outlook could revolutionize Europe's economic pat-

tern. This turned out to be one of the most accurate judgments ever made in Washington; largely freed from the dead
hand of the past by the catastrophe of war, many Europeans
completely reshaped their economic concepts along much
more American lines. Enabled—actually forced—to start
from scratch in building their factories, European entre-
preneurs were free to introduce the most advanced production techniques, in many cases surpassing their American
models in efficiency and rationality.

From this generally optimistic evaluation Great Britain
must be largely excepted. Britain had not suffered as great
(or as visible) an economic loss as had most of the continental states, and therefore entered the postwar world with
substantially the same production plant it had brought into
the twentieth century. In addition, Britain lacked what
some wags identified as the priceless advantage of having
lost the war. As a victor, Britain was less inclined to take a
completely fresh look at the requirements of the national
economy, a look that was essential to any major overhaul.
Instead Britain assumed (in the face of considerable contrary evidence) that events would move substantially as they
had before the war. The British people and their government were to suffer for this oversight before too many years
had passed.

United States interest in restoring Europe's economic
vigor focused on the already industrialized nations and was
less intense in the agricultural sector or in such states as
Italy, Greece, or Portugal, where industry was not so highly
developed. Even in these areas, however, the massive American effort was not without significant result. The Marshall
Plan is as gratefully recalled today in southern Italy as in
the Ruhr, although perhaps with less objective economic
reason.

A third European failing that the United States set out to

cure was military weakness, identified both in terms of
Europe's incapacity to defend itself against external aggression and its inability to project military power beyond its
own immediate area. The war had ended with Britain the
only non-communist state in Europe with any military pretensions at all. By 1948, however, even London's brave
front had collapsed, and the United States was forced to assume major British commitments in the eastern Mediter-
ranean. Nowhere in Western Europe was there any indigenous military power. Except for the few American occupation troops in Germany, Europe lay all but defenseless
before the Soviet threat.

As Americans looked at the problem in both its regional
and its world-wide context, there seemed only one hopeful
route to restore Europe's military position to a safe and
feasible basis. The United States felt that it must firmly ally
itself with as many European states as possible, then lead
the way to a new and higher level of military preparedness.
It was clear from the outset that the American role was to
be a major one, both in determining the type and magnitude
of military establishment that each of the European allies
was to construct and in formulating the common strategy
the European-American camp was to follow in confronting
the Soviet Union and its bloc.

The key to the combination lay in early and extensive
West German rearmament on conditions acceptable to
Western Europe and not overly provocative to the Soviet
Union. The United States started to work in this direction
as soon as the Cold War began in earnest. The first great
breakthrough occurred in 1948 with the establishment of
the West German government; the first setback (although
temporary) came in 1954 with the failure of the European
Defense Community. Fulfillment was actually achieved in
1955 when West Germany entered NATO. Today, most

Americans count the successful yet controlled rearmament of West Germany as one of the major diplomatic triumphs of the postwar era.

Although military revival was a considerable success in the case of West Germany, the same cannot be said of the other nations of Western Europe. Neither France nor Britain proved capable of meeting (or being willing to meet) American expectations—or even their own minimum commitments—in the military field. Since 1951 the United States has constantly advocated a higher level of armament and preparedness than its European allies have in fact maintained, with a predictable harvest of reciprocal bad feelings. Even in Germany, as a matter of fact, the military rationale has not always been happily received.

When all was said and done, however, Europe's failings in political organization, economic structure, and military power in the postwar world were in American eyes only symptomatic of a deeper malaise. Europe's major problem, it seemed, was spiritual: Europeans, bereft of faith and self-confidence, had lost their capacity to deal realistically and effectively with their own problems. Physical, emotional, and moral exhaustion appeared to characterize the European scene after the war, in sharp contrast to the vigor and pride that had been the continent's hallmarks during its heyday.

To the United States in the late 1940's, major foreign policy decisions were admittedly complex in an operational sense, but conceptually they were refreshingly simple. Containment was not an especially subtle idea, nor did it conceal very many unperceived ramifications—or at least so it seemed at the time. American response to the spiritual failure of Europe was similarly direct and uncomplicated, derived as it was from the dynamic premise of the Cold War. If Europeans were too fatigued or too shortsighted to identify their proper course in a drastically changed world, then the United States had to set them on the appropriate track and keep them moving in the right direction.

This is the genesis of the American mission of "leadership," a role that offered much gratification to the United States (as well as not a little disillusionment in later years). Again the point must be made clear: at least in the beginning, America seized the duty of leading Europe to a new world role for the noblest and most disinterested of reasons. Americans were certain that a once-proud Europe would never settle for mere survival; nor, for that matter, would economic and political recovery be adequate. Europe, Americans reasoned, needed to rediscover a purpose and a mission in the world. Two historical trends thus intersected neatly: America, equipped with a new international mission but needing allies, encountered a Europe with great potential but no real purpose. By serving the cause of freedom in support of American policy, Europe would find its soul while the United States gained the assistance it needed. Both peoples would be satisfied and fulfilled.

The strange vagaries of the U.S. leadership role form one of the controlling themes of this book. It is a historical fact that Europe recovered from its exhaustion somewhat more rapidly than the United States had expected. It is also a matter of record that this great revival—one of the major events of world history during the past two decades—did not follow the lines hoped for and encouraged by Washington, and that this *contretemps* is one of the major difficulties in European-American relations today.

Exhaustion was a reality in many parts of Europe in 1946, as any American who was there at the time can testify. But the march of subsequent events suggests that Europe's fatigue was the natural and predictable result of six years of devastating war that followed a decade of economic depression and international crisis, rather than any failure of moral or nervous fiber in the population generally. Europeans, it turned out, were able to discover their own purposes and move quickly to their fulfillment, leaving the United States with the sense of having performed a valuable service that unfortunately produced no net gains.

The postwar American image of Europe, therefore, was (and, to a major extent, is today) largely the result of a reversal of the one that had prevailed through most of American history. Where Americans had once felt inferior to Europeans, they came to feel superior; where they had once sought to avoid involvement, they came to assume a direct and active role; where they had once feared, they came to patronize and—to put it bluntly—condescend. The United States set out to preserve Europe from the threat of Soviet conquest, but even more to save Europe from the consequences of its own incompetence and bad luck.

To this image of a Europe politically disunited, economically backward, militarily powerless, and psychically ravished, the United States has remained faithful. When American officials insist, as they often do, that in European-American relations and in the security problem of the West "nothing fundamental has changed" since 1949, they are testifying eloquently to their own faith in this old image. Whatever changes have taken place since are dismissed as peripheral or irrelevant. The consequences of this admirable consistency of viewpoint may be seen in the present state of European-American relations.

Europe, America and the "Free World"

In attempting to identify and define the premises of the American approach to Europe since 1945, one primary factor must be kept firmly in mind. From 1946 to 1966 the United States has perceived only one real issue in Europe: the defense of the entire continent against a Soviet armed attack, internal communist subversion, or both. This is to say that the entire content of American policy in the region has been determined—or at least materially affected by—the concepts and requirements of an active Cold War.

At the very beginning the United States had hoped to give its policy a broader base. The Marshall Plan was originally unveiled by the Secretary of State as a move positively in American interests, essential regardless of the state of Soviet-American relations. Public apathy and incipient opposition in Congress soon persuaded the executive branch, however, to portray the European Recovery Program as a follow-up to the militantly anti-communist Truman Doctrine of 1947. Americans both in and out of Congress were prepared to accept this point of view, and the Marshall Plan was passed as an overtly anti-Soviet measure, part of a rapidly escalating Cold War. As European economic recovery became part of the global struggle against communism, the American attitude toward European questions of all sorts became fixed and all but irrevocable.

During the late 1940's the United States more or less officially reduced its position vis-à-vis Europe to a series of assumptions, simple and straightforward in their effect and capable of providing a base for policy decisions of all sorts. These may be formulated as follow:

1. Europe is the primary target of communist expansion because of its inherent value and its inability to defend itself.

2. Europe is so strategically, economically, and politically critical that it must be held by the United States at all costs.

3. The Soviet Union will move to conquer Western Europe the moment the strategic situation becomes sufficiently favorable.

4. To deny the Soviet Union this opportunity, the United States must man the front-line defenses of Europe itself

while building a solid front of democratic and anti-communist nations.

5. With its great resources, heavy risks, and secure base at home, the United States, in logic and in justice, is entitled to the leadership of all states actively involved in the defense of Western Europe.

Fortified by these propositions, long regarded as self-evident, Americans have had a useful yardstick for measuring and evaluating each intra-European or transatlantic development. The Soviet-American struggle—defined always in terms of its original, black-and-white Stalinist formulation—has been the touchstone of desirable evolution in the West. Whatever (from the American point of view) strengthened the anti-communist camp in its capacity to deter or resist Soviet attack was considered a "good thing"; whatever threatened to weaken the determination or the capability of the Western alliance to confront Moscow was denounced and, if possible, nullified by Washington.

Realism forces a further admission: by prolonging the Cold-War context of European-American relations, the United States extends the era of its extensive control over Europe's destiny. This is by no means to echo the heavy-handed charges often made by de Gaulle's France that the United States seeks to maintain something called "hegemony" over the states of Western Europe, but only to emphasize the obvious. As a newly great power, the United States naturally seeks maximum control over events in which it takes part, and resists any attempt to narrow that range of free decision. As long as the Cold War argument succeeds in maintaining a major American posture in Europe, it will continue to be used.

In view of the reluctance and the hesitation with which Americans originally approached Europe, it is remarkable how quickly they came to enjoy their mission of defending and tending their charges. The United States found something peculiarly satisfying about the extensive arrangements, institutions, and organizations that rapidly sprang up to implement its original commitment. Americans fell to congratulating themselves after 1948 and 1949 for the "wisdom," the "sincerity," the "forcefulness," and the "generosity" of their new policies in Western Europe. The nation quickly became proud of the speed and magnitude of its acceptance of the challenge of history, and felt that the gratitude and support it expected in return were no more than its just due.

A central element in the new American rationale was the concept of the "free world." The bipolar Cold War demanded a dichotomous view of the political universe. Stalin argued that the world was made up of the communist and the non-communist camps; the United States went him one better by dividing it into the communist and the *anti*-communist blocs. All who had not committed themselves to communist principles, therefore, were united in their determination to resist Moscow's incursions; the United States, as the Soviet Union's principal opponent, and presumably as the one state with the wisdom and the power to play the part, was the natural leader of all free men. This massive bloc, united neither by force nor by a rigid ideology, but rather by dedication to a common set of principles, was the "free world."

The states of Western Europe were to be the first and most important recruits to this policy. Washington accorded them a special place in its thinking, counted on them for extensive and devoted service, and has been all the more sharply disappointed in their failure fully to justify American efforts and measure up to American expectations. Selfish or shortsighted behavior is normal among communists, and is to be expected and tolerated among neutrals or unstable allies; but for fellow members of the Western core of the "free world" to be false to the noble principles of morality and freedom has been a heavy burden indeed for Americans to bear.

Accepting the communists' simplistic definition of the international environment, including a dominant common interest of all states hostile to Soviet expansion, allowed the United States to develop a powerful system of logic. To begin with, since everyone identified the problem in much the same way, it was no great effort to assume that all members of the free world agreed that a single, well-organized, and unified policy in opposition to communism was necessary, feasible, and desirable. It was only a short step to go further and assume that all also shared the primary purpose of frustrating the Soviet challenge, individually as well as collectively. Each would be willing to subordinate lesser or competing national aims as long as necessary.

One more element completed this American thesis. With so much ideological and political consensus undergirding the free world, questions of internal organization or procedure were assumed to be only minor difficulties. Efficiency would be the criterion: in establishing structures and selecting means, methods would be adopted that performed the common task with the greatest speed, economy, or simplicity. In so enormous and well-intentioned an enterprise, mere national biases in favor of leadership roles or prestige could be dismissed as beneath notice and, in view of the scope and nature of the challenge, were furthermore unlikely to be present. Harmony-in-unity was the supposed controlling characteristic of free-world policy.

Thus, the U.S. saw the free world—and especially its European-American core—as a massive coalition of free peoples and more or less democratic governments who agreed with the United States and with each other on all important questions (that is, on all questions relating to the threat of communism and the strategy for its defeat—for these were, by definition, the only important ones). Ideological solidarity within the free world was assumed, as was a substantial degree of political symmetry in foreign policy. In the realm of action, the obvious weakness of the minor members of the free world in 1947 assured the leadership role of the United States.

This historical fact gave the notion of the free world an American dimension. The United States, moving actively into the breach left by the inability of its associates to act unilaterally, undertook the defense of the entire free world within the guise of containment. The free world first became a policy reality in the European context; the idea received both its greatest development and its severest tests in Atlantic relations.

The concept of the free world and the sweep of American alliance policy—although thrown into sharpest relief in the pattern of European-American relations—reinforces this basis of inequality. The unity of purpose linking all members of the coalition, of which so much is made in American rhetoric, really requires a sharp differentiation of roles. All members of the free world may indeed be alike in their dedication to freedom and justice, but this (if true) is the only sense in which they are to be considered equal. In all operational aspects, inequality is the keynote.

This is why the United States is so insistent on efficiency and rationality as organizing concepts of the free world in the realm of action. In this context "efficiency" means allocating tasks and responsibilities among the members according to their respective capabilities, with each nation doing what it is best fitted to do. With each playing an appropriate role, each thus contributes to the common effort and at the same time gains satisfaction from being required to do what it does best in any case.

Still within the frame of efficiency, one question remains to be asked: What is the best—i.e., the most efficient—way of identifying problems, formulating tasks, and allocating responsibilities for the free world? Several alternatives are theoretically possible. The democratic orientation of the free-world coalition would suggest a system of permanent consultation among all members, with decisions made by more or less formalized voting procedures. Such an arrangement was actually built into NATO. But if one grants that military defense against a communist threat was and is still the major purpose of the free world, democratic decision-making procedures are neither most efficient nor most controllable. Some simpler and more reliable way of making Western policy would seem more suitable for an alliance that might have to fight for its life at any moment.

Here again the United States was ready with a thesis suited to the occasion and neatly grounded on its own major premises. Since the free world was united in a common mission, and since the United States had (and has) the central and largest role in implementing that mission, the most efficient and effective way to make policy and to apportion tasks within the alliance system—especially in crisis situations—was to allow the United States to do it alone.

To Americans this was both logical and just. It was inconceivable that the national interest of the United States could ever be separated from the common interest of the free world, since American purposes were nothing less than the welfare of all free men. Suspicions to the contrary were inherently unworthy. Wasn't the United States the creator of the alliance in the first place, and wasn't America the last best hope of free men everywhere? Most Americans

are still persuaded that the interests of all their allies—
their *true* interests, that is, as distinguished from their
short-term, selfish, and narrow preoccupations—are perfectly safe in American hands.

The American approach permitted consultation and
even formalized decision-making, if not carried too far.
Consultation was looked upon primarily as an instrument
by which the American position could be explained to
poorly informed or recalcitrant allies, to set their doubts
at rest; common policy was a euphemism for the acceptance
of American-inspired designs and techniques. There has
never been any clear prediction of what the American response might be if the United States were outvoted or over-
ruled in a free-world assembly; from the general tenor of
official American comment, one is tempted to infer that
the United States has never admitted such a possibility as
sufficiently realistic to justify advance planning.

All these general propositions about the nature and dynamics of the free world today have a universal application, but it is important to remember that they were first
expressed, refined, and applied in Europe. The American
point of view on world affairs in the postwar era was indelibly marked by its early experiments in transatlantic
cooperation. So solidly were the lessons learned in Europe
in 1949 to 1952 that their inapplicability to non-European
areas has been only slowly perceived by the United States
(and even more slowly admitted). Their decreasing relevance to the European situation, of course, is still denied
emphatically in most official quarters in Washington.

The Failure of the Image

The postwar image of Western Europe accepted so unquestioningly by Americans for two decades has fallen alarmingly out of touch with reality. The peoples and the governments of Western Europe no longer think and act as Americans assume they should; instead, what was once a familiar and reassuring landscape, across which the United States could move easily, has become a sinister, booby-trapped environment in which Americans find themselves at a continuous disadvantage. As a result of the failure of the American image of Western Europe, American public attitudes are being repeatedly lacerated, American policies resisted, and American initiatives rebuffed.

What has gone wrong with the image? How is Europe today so different from what Americans expect and so changed from the grouping of natural and harmonious allies the United States succored and organized in the late 1940's?

In the first place, the major failure of the American image is that it was from the beginning far too optimistic. Operating under a full head of emotional steam at a moment of major crisis, the United States jumped to several extravagant conclusions about the kind of relationship it was forging with its new allies in Europe. Europe and America were, after all, not the soul-mates early American Cold War policy had postulated; the arrangements between them were not the consummation of a historical process. Instead, this was no more than a political *mariage de convenance*—in other words, no different in essence from other cooperative undertakings of sovereign states.

Related to the extravagant optimism of the American image has been the innocent and well-meaning, but nevertheless deadly, egocentrism around which it was built. The United States constructed a vision of Europe as a necessary, yet definitely secondary, complement to the unique world role the United States believed itself destined to play. For the United States to lead, followers were necessary: Europe filled the bill. It was easy to assume European agreement with the American view of the overall mission of the anti-communist camp. Whatever the United States felt Europe *should* be, think, and feel as an associate in the common Cold War, Americans quickly concluded was the way Europeans *actually* were, thought, and felt.

Probably the central American misapprehension of the European phenomenon was the idea of what might be called the "new normality" of European-American relations. Sometime in the late 1940's the United States came to terms with its own strength and Europe's glaring weakness, and erected a theory and a philosophy on that ground. The relative roles of Europe and the United States during the early days of the Cold War were analyzed not as a temporary reversal of status and function brought about by the fortunes of war, but rather as the culmination of an historic process that began at Plymouth and Jamestown in the early seventeenth century and reached its peak with the North Atlantic Treaty. American protection and European dependence, American universalism and European regionalism, American centrality and European peripherality were the new norms of Western political life. They were the new permanent features of world affairs.

As early as 1949 many Europeans did not agree with the American assumptions. They saw their weakness as transitory, a condition to be eliminated as soon as possible on the way to restoring Europe's own independent and central role in the world. To the extent that Americans paid any attention to repeated European declarations of this intent during the 1950's and early 1960's (a period in which one Asian crisis succeeded another with bewildering rapidity), they tended to tolerate rather than respond to them.

European resentment of this new normality was dismissed as a natural but essentially irrelevant digression. The peoples of the Old World, Americans reasoned, were of course finding their transition into permanent secondary status very difficult to accept. The United States could afford to tolerate these effusions, at least to a point; the inexorabilities of power relations would inevitably "bring Europe to its senses." In the meantime a posture of patient firmness by the United States, marked by affection and solicitude but free from any excessive weak-kneed pandering to outraged European sensibilities, would smooth and expedite the historical transformation of Europe from its lost grandeur to its new status as a junior partner of the champion of the West.

Another hasty conclusion that went into the image was the doctrine of the "common mission," essential to the global policy the United States attempted to build during the 1950's. The peoples of Europe were obviously opposed to being taken over by the Soviet Union, and since the United States shared this feeling, a common mission quite obviously existed in 1948 and still exists today. But the rhetoric of a bipolar Cold War never persuaded many Europeans, and to move from joint defense on the continent to a common European-American policy to contain communism everywhere in the world has been too great a leap for Europe to take—even though it has long been urged by Washington. The common global mission of Europe and the United States has never been a reality.

In the first place, Europe generally never agreed with the United States about the nature of the Soviet threat and refused to accept the American definition of the problem as controlling on everyone. As our subsequent analysis of common defense policy and its problems will show, Europeans by and large have never felt that the danger from Moscow was as great or as imminent as the United States has steadily insisted. As a result, they have obstructed and frustrated American plans, failed to meet the commitments the United States has wheedled out of them, and retained an undesirable (from the American point of view) autonomy in dealing with the Soviet Union and China.

In the second place, the American doctrine of the common mission insisted that the successful prosecution of the Cold War was the most important single element of foreign policy. The Cold War occupied first place in American thinking, and the United States demanded that it be equally important to all its associates. Few assumptions of national policy have ever had so shaky a foundation or enjoyed less fulfillment in the real world.

Europe entered into alliance with the United States simply because it felt it needed American protection; Washington's institutional arrangements were no more than part of the price Europeans had to pay for the American guarantee. Europe, in other words, was serving its several national interests (and, to an increasing extent, its regional interest) by accepting American assistance. In no way did Europe deceive the United States on this point. So long as Europe felt the Soviet threat to be a major one, it would be met by common action with the United States. Its subsequent decline, however, has afforded European statesmen the opportunity they have long sought to initiate major policies springing from indigenous interests and aspirations.

Thus, the common interest in European-American relations has been in fact confined to Europe's concern with its own safety, defense, and prosperity. So long as American policy advances the interests of Europeans, they will cooperate; when it does not, they will either ignore or obstruct it. With the rhetoric of the Cold War and the global implications of the American outlook, Europeans have little intrinsic involvement except in two special ways. They view with increasing alarm extensive American forays into faraway places as degrading the integrity of America's pledge to them; some of them also have interests in certain non-European areas which they are reluctant to permit Washington to tamper with and perhaps to prejudice unfavorably. Otherwise, so long as the United States does not by its militancy provoke a world nuclear war, they are content to permit Americans the psychic satisfaction of crusading against communism. They ask only that they not be included in the enterprise.

Still another failure of the American image of Europe lies in American expectations that Europe has been, still is, and will eternally remain "grateful" for American assistance, and that this sense of obligation can be counted on— if logic and the spirit of justice should fail—finally to bring Europe to support American policies, either in Europe or elsewhere. As European-American relations have grown more tendentious in recent years, and as the reluctance of certain European states to subordinate themselves to American pre-eminence has become more obvious, accusations of "ingratitude" have become increasingly common in the United States.

For what, as the United States sees it, should Europe be grateful? First, for the end of American isolationism and the active entry of the United States into intra-European affairs. Second, for the American role in salvaging two world wars when they seemed to be slipping out of control (although how this affects German thinking is never made explicit). Third, for the Marshall Plan, the North Atlantic Treaty, the nuclear umbrella Washington holds over Europe, and for the key role America has accorded Europe in its global planning for the Cold War. In other words, Europe ought to be grateful permanently for the American presence in Europe, for past beneficence as well as the expectation of continued interest and assistance.

All expectations of gratitude, it must be emphasized, flow from the American self-image in the Cold War. The United States tends—at least on its occasional peaks of rhetorical euphoria—to see itself not as a single nation-state serving its own interests, but rather as the chosen instrument of a great historical force. Thus, American policy in Europe has from the beginning been literally extraordinary, a disinterested but mighty effort aimed at the common good and springing from philanthropy and a stern sense of duty, in approximately equal measure.

All this, it must be repeated, is perfectly clear to most Americans, and they are at a loss to explain why it is not just as clear to Europeans as well. In point of fact, the European explanation of the American presence in Europe has always been much simpler, much more realistic, and—from the European point of view—more complimentary to American intelligence. Europe, while downgrading American philanthropy and American disinterestedness, has simply assumed from the beginning that the United States is playing power politics by classical rules, and that the ideological and metaphysical elements of America's apologia are only the necessary trappings of a realistic policy.

If the United States is playing power politics, then any discussion of so apolitical a term as "gratitude" defies good common sense. The United States chose to enter both world wars not because of any desire to "save" Europe but to defend its own national interest in the European balance of power; the United States defends Europe today against Soviet attack and communist subversion for the same reason. Why, Europeans ask, should they be grateful because several sets of American politicians turned out to be devoted servants of the national interest of the United States? That Europe benefited from American interest is both obvious and fortunate, but the American interpretation of interest is susceptible to change at any moment. Gratitude for past assistance, Europe insists, never provides a useful guide for decisions in power politics.

All this has been extremely frustrating for the United States. It may be, as critics point out, that American professions of disinterestedness and dedication are no more than rationalizations for power interests that are no less powerful for being concealed even from the American people themselves. Yet, even after two decades of the Cold War, the concept of "naked power" still repels and appalls Americans, and the nation has always sought some higher and more moral rationale for its efforts than the simple calculus of force and expediency. There is no doubt that America would be delighted to feel that its policy in Europe is indeed prompted by some loftier end.

This is the major role—at least for the general public— played by the image of Europe for the past two decades. No aspect of the global policy of the United States since 1945 has been more of a break with past tradition than American involvement in Europe. Some overview of the nature of the environment, some myth of mission and purpose, and some rationalizing formula for the possibility of frustration and failure have been necessary to structure public responses to and acceptance of new departures and major crises. As such, the image has served a useful purpose throughout its effective life.

But governments, presumably wiser and more sophisticated than the publics they serve, are all too often the prisoners of a mass consensus they originally helped to create. Today the United States is in this predicament: the image of Europe has played the American people false. Policy is at a dead end, and new initiatives are all but impossible until they can be centered upon a new focus. The unrealistic expectations stirred by the original postwar view of Europe remain to plague American policy-makers, while the realities of the situation go unserved and almost unnoticed. It is time to develop a new American image of Europe.

Chapter Three
The Foundations:
Defense, Alliance,
Leadership

In the preceding chapter we sketched the psychic bases of American policy in postwar Europe. Responding to the image of Europe that prevailed in the United States at the end of the war and that has continued to the present, the American government has been nothing if not consistent. American policy toward Western Europe has been built on theoretical formulations that have been implemented with great persistence, not a little ingenuity, and considerable rhetoric. All of them are authentic expressions of the American interpretation of the national mission in the European environment; all of them, therefore, share in the strengths and weaknesses of the original premises upon which the United States has steadily relied.

Three separate lines of theoretical (or, more properly, doctrinal) development can be identified in the grand design of American policy in and toward Europe. The first concerns the problems of the defense of Central and Western Europe against a Soviet attack. The second deals with the nature and dynamics of the Atlantic alliance, and particularly with its major manifestation, the North Atlantic Treaty Organization. The third involves American political and military leadership of its European associates, both in terms of regional preoccupations and of the larger mission of the free world in the Cold War. Out of the American position on these crucial issues has flowed a large part of the controversy and misunderstanding that have impaired the viability of the great coalition.

Before we turn to an analysis of these doctrines, one preliminary point should be made. Although in logic and in fact the three foundation stones of American policy are intellectually separable, very frequently discussions (in the United States and on a transatlantic basis) of particular issues tend to slip from one realm to another. Arguments about defense policy cannot—and should not—be decided by emotional explanations of America's historic role as the leader of the West; controversies over the nature of the alliance do not yield to elaborate and abstruse doctrines of deterrence. When one is dealing with defense, he should argue strategic concepts; when he is arguing alliance dynamics, he should stick to what history and common sense teach about the nature of coalitions. To do otherwise is to confuse hopelessly a situation already sufficiently complex.

The American Doctrine of European Defense

Early in the Cold War and very shortly after the United States actively entered the European arena, the basic strategic ingredient in the European situation was the danger of Soviet aggression. Washington soon reached a correspondingly basic decision that the defense of the West was to be based on a "forward strategy." This meant that the line NATO would defend against a Soviet assault would be in the zone of initial contact—along the Iron Curtain and the Elbe River—rather than along the Rhine after giving up almost all of Central Europe to Soviet forces. This decision carried important and far-reaching implications for future doctrine and policy.

The most important result of the idea of a forward strategy was the inevitability of active German participation in defense planning. Without West German forces, resistance along the Iron Curtain was impossible; with them, however, a very flexible strategic posture was—at least in theory—possible for the allied forces. A second consequence of the original decision was the long and inconclusive quarrel over force levels, command, and national units that has raged within NATO throughout its history and continues unabated today.

With its genius for phrasemaking, American policy soon provided a verbal tag for its theory of NATO defense. As gradually refined by official formulation, American doctrine came to be known as the "sword and the shield." The sword was the nuclear retaliatory capability of the alliance (largely an American monopoly) that performed a double mission: it deterred the Soviet Union from attacking, and it was the main instrument of reprisal if the Soviets refused to be deterred. The shield embraced the land, sea, and air forces of NATO in Europe, whose task was to hold Soviet forces in check while the sword demolished the Soviet heartland, denying Moscow the possibility of the quick victory in Europe that alone could make the gamble of total war attractive.

This strategy became feasible after West Germany entered NATO in 1955 and began actively to rearm. It remained the controlling and almost unchallenged American doctrine until well into the 1960's. Implicit in the concept of the sword and the shield, however, were several pre-conditions upon which the entire theory rested.

The first requirement was that American nuclear superiority remain sufficiently convincing to retain the sword of final decision. The second was that the major members of NATO specialize their roles, with the United States caring for the sword and the Europeans bearing the major burden of raising and maintaining the shield. The third was that NATO forces of all types continue under a unified command, which meant (since American strategic nuclear power was required by Congress to remain entirely under unilateral American control) permanent American domination of NATO military matters.

Obviously, the first requirement for the validity of the sword-and-shield doctrine—the continued nuclear supremacy of the United States—has been drastically compromised. The Soviet Union has made massive strides in the development of strategic weapons, and today an uneasy balance governs the relationship between the two giants. U.S. nuclear capability today is generally agreed to exceed the Soviets' by a comfortable margin—comfortable, that is, in terms of its capacity to deter Soviet missile attack. But the lead the United States enjoys is completely inadequate to justify the dream that even a pre-emptive American nuclear strike on the Soviet Union could produce victory at low cost, or short of desperate total war.

The second precondition, the specialization in roles and missions, has also run afoul of history. The rough classification of NATO forces into conventional and expendable European infantry and artillery, on the one hand, and strategic, behind-the-lines American missilemen, on the other, has always contained the germs of invidious comparisons and of European resentment of second-class status. France, for example, has never accepted NATO's mission as controlling itself. The overall force levels of the shield have never been reached in terms of fully operational units in the field, and the United States has constantly been obliged to exhort, cajole, assist, and on occasion to threaten its allies in order to bring them close to meeting their commitments—and usually has, furthermore, suffered frustration for its pains.

The third requirement, unity of command, has had the stormiest history, having been the focus of the most serious disagreements in NATO. The sword-and-shield concept is cast in an image of unity; both types of military action (nuclear and conventional) flow from a single strategic appraisal and are parts of a single operational design. Barred by law and by policy from sharing its nuclear power with any other state, the United States has from time to time asserted what it has assumed from the beginning: the inevitability of its right to command the entire military apparatus of the alliance.

If the decision to launch nuclear weapons must be exclusively an American one, then both military logic and common sense dictate that full control over the military situation be finally vested in American hands. In practice, the Supreme Allied Commander in Europe (SACEUR) has always been an American, and American doctrine has emphasized his role while minimizing the collective features of the alliance.

To these calculated strategic arguments, the United States has added a separate plea for retention of command unity: justice and fair play. As the nation that contributes the bulk of the muscle to NATO, as the nation that has twice in this century come to the rescue of Europe, as the nation with the heaviest responsibilities in the fight against communism, and as the nation whose advice and support have saved Europe from Moscow, America feels that it deserves the loudest voice and the final power of decision on basic questions. It needs scarcely to be emphasized here that this entire line of argument is a pat example of the confusion of issues that was noted above, and as such it has received short shrift from Europe.

The various American attempts to salvage the sword and shield in the face of eroding circumstances will be examined in detail below. Even more important here, however, is the fact that—in a sudden, unpredictable, and extreme fashion that many Europeans think of as "typically American"— the United States in the 1960's has stood this theory of European defense substantially on its head. Under the inspiration of President John F. Kennedy, and thanks to the new breed of analysts in the Pentagon (the "whiz kids"), the roles of the sword and the shield have been completely reversed in American thinking.

Contemporary American military doctrine contends that the new technology has revolutionized the principles of procuring, deploying, and using modern weapons. Most important is the stalemate in strategic nuclear weapons; by the time the Kennedy administration had completed its reassessment of the situation, American strategic nuclear capability had lost its role as the striking sword of the alliance and had instead become only a deterrent shield. This proposition forced a corresponding reversal of roles for NATO's conventional forces: today official doctrine considers them the sword of victory.

The official downgrading of strategic nuclear power is demonstrated most clearly by the adoption of a "counterforce" strategy of targeting Soviet missile potential rather than aiming at widespread destruction of Russian population centers. The new military emphasis is instead on flexibility (especially in the area of less-than-total capability), programmed response at a great range of levels, extensive contingency planning, and an elaborate command structure to safeguard against escalation. The announced objective of this repatterning of the entire rationale of European defense is to avoid either a "knee-jerk" response to a Soviet provocation that might plunge the world into nuclear holocaust, or else the paralysis that might occur if nothing short of total response were available.

This last point opens an even more fundamental issue in defense strategy for the entire Atlantic community: the nature of deterrence and how best to dissuade the Soviet Union from launching an attack. The United States has built its strategic estimate on the premise that—at least for planning purposes—the intentions of the Soviets are synonymous with their capabilities; in other words, the Soviets will always act as aggressively as they feel the situation permits. Thus, deterrence for the United States is a constantly active problem, one of restraining Soviet invasions that are always prepared to roll at the moment the West relaxes its vigilance. No European state—not even West Germany, the one that comes closest to doing so—accepts this premise as a basis for planning, and this discontinuity of strategic vision has contributed largely to intra-alliance disagreements over defense matters.

Another complicating element has been an unfortunate confusion between doctrines of deterrence and doctrines of response. There is an important conceptual difference: deterrence aims to prevent an attack; response aims to defeat it. Response capability may (but also may not) be an effective deterrent, but other factors contribute as well. Probably the most important of these is uncertainty: an enemy who is not certain of the West's response finds his decision-making much more difficult—and making a decision to attack difficult or impossible is the aim of any deterrent strategy.

All this is relevant to American formulas of deterrence. The best known of all—at least in its popularized and anathematized version—is the so-called "massive retaliation" thesis, indelibly identified with the late John Foster

Dulles. In spite of the obloquy that clouds his name and his doctrine, Secretary of State Dulles never argued for massive retaliation to any Soviet pinprick. His theory was much more subtle: he warned any potential aggressor that the United States could *not* be counted upon to respond in kind and at the place of the attack. Instead, the United States reserved the right to "retaliate massively at places and times" of American choosing. This was not a strategy of response, but a strategy of deterrence. Its object was not to bury the Soviets under a fiery rain of nuclear weapons, but to dissuade Moscow from attempting reckless ventures.

Massive retaliation was systematically attacked throughout the Eisenhower years by platoons of critics who argued that the threat to destroy the world in response to minor Soviet probes was simply not credible, and that the United States had denied itself any options other than total war. That these arguments were generally based upon a caricature of the Dulles theory rather than upon the doctrine itself, and that they mistook deterrence for response, was never regarded as particularly relevant. The Kennedy administration took office pledged to replace the doctrine of massive retaliation with a more credible and workable theory of defense.

This eventually surfaced as "flexible response." In essence, flexible response promised a spectrum of American reactions to Soviet attack, with the kind of retaliation to be determined by the extent and severity of the onslaught itself —"making the punishment fit the crime."

This was, however, not a deterrent strategy at all; although making total war less likely, it also—as its supporters admitted early in the 1960's—made less-than-total ("limited") war more probable than had the discredited doctrine of massive retaliation. The Kennedy administration speedily rectified this error shortly after taking power. The new doctrine, while promising an almost absolute flex-

ibility in response, firmly reserved the right of nuclear retaliation to any provocation—a somewhat more delicate
way of putting the essential point of the Dulles theory.

Thus, the United States today hopes, at least in Europe,
to have the best of both worlds: it retains the notion of
massive retaliation and forces a heavy burden of uncertainty on Soviet decision-makers, while it also maintains a
vast family of responses at a lower range and level, each
protected by a built-in pause for evaluation. From Washington the situation seems as stabilized as it ever can be.

Not so, however, in Europe, and here lies a good bit of
the difficulty. By and large, Europeans—especially conti-
nentals like the West Germans and the French—were
pleased with massive retaliation as a deterrent theory, and
also as a theory of response. Few Europeans ever took
seriously the fighting ability of NATO's conventional forces
or the likelihood that a subnuclear war in Europe would
leave anything worth worrying about after the fighting
stopped. To an extent almost unsuspected by the United
States, lost as it was in elaborate forward-defense tactical
plans, Europe has from the beginning placed its own hope
for defense in deterrence rather than in response. Only if
Moscow could be persuaded not to attack in the first place
could Europe be saved; the continent could not afford to be
liberated for the third time in the twentieth century.

Massive retaliation, therefore, suited European interests
perfectly. The Dulles doctrine placed all of America's resources at the defense of Europe, available in full the
moment the first Soviet soldier crossed the Iron Curtain
with hostile intent. The failure of deterrence meant the end
of all rational planning.

Official American interment of massive retaliation and
its replacement by flexible response brought no chorus of
huzzas from Europe, which saw a limited Soviet attack being greeted by a limited Western response—another World

War II with the added destructiveness of new weapons of conventional ground warfare. Furthermore, the built-in pause in response, of which the United States was so proud, meant to Europeans only that the U.S. was prepared to grant Soviet attackers undefined—but perhaps extensive— slices of European territory while Washington was making up its mind that the attack was legitimate. Flexible response is far from popular in Western Europe today.

The United States has sought to assure its allies (who are also its protégés) that the differences between massive retaliation and flexible response are more apparent than real. The pauses, it is alleged, will be short; the United States will not permit Soviet conquest of any considerable portions of NATO territory. The U.S. nuclear guarantee, moreover, is not conditional. But on the central issue, Washington is adamant: the United States will never overtly return to the image of massive retaliation.

This is where the matter stands today. The United States, still committed to the idea that the Soviet military threat is as serious as ever—or even more so—has developed a defense doctrine that does not persuade Europeans. They cannot believe that the United States is serious in insisting that NATO's conventional forces are to be the sword of final victory over the huge armies of the Soviet bloc, nor are they confident that the United States will use its strategic nuclear capability fully to deter or to retaliate against a Soviet thrust. American doctrine, however much it glorifies tactical flexibility, is discouragingly inflexible on these points. American spokesmen have done little more in recent years than argue that the controlling theory of allied defense in Europe does not really mean what it says!

One final point. In its dealings with its European allies, the United States insists that "nothing fundamental has changed" with respect to the Soviet challenge to Europe. But in direct bilateral relationships with the Kremlin, the

United States has been making serious (and commendable) efforts to "build bridges" to the East and to establish an easier and more manageable climate of Soviet-American relations. These two positions, the intra-alliance and the Soviet-American, are reconcilable, but the United States has not made as convincing a case for reconciling them as it might have. The result has been natural: Europeans wonder if the United States is actually sincere in describing the Soviet menace, and from time to time they take pleasure in ascribing sinister motives to American moves in either area.

Probably the major difficulty with American defense doctrine for Europe has been its heavily technical, professional, and non-political orientation. From a purely military point of view, it is permissible—often necessary—to assume that enemy capabilities do in fact equal enemy intentions, and to develop contingency plans on the basis that the adversary will always act with maximum hostility. But the problems of the defense of Europe, particularly in view of the extremely complex political issues involved, have never been purely military. They have always had major ingredients of political judgment to which American policy-makers have not been adequately sensitive. To a proud and newly self-assertive European state (for example, France) to be lectured by the United States on the evils of communism, and to be told that all necessary political wisdom resides in Washington, is an exquisitely annoying experience. Repetitions of it have not improved relations.

Thus, American concern with efficiency, rationality, unity, and completeness in making defense plans for Europe has collided squarely with many European preferences for a less structured and more autonomous relationship. Theories that seem irrefutable in a Pentagon briefing room turn out to be almost impotent when urged on stubborn (or even merely selfish) European governments. Specialization in roles and missions is logical and efficient; but when Europeans complain that practically it would mean enormous European casualty lists while American forces would suffer proportionately much less, the United States has no answer—except that this is the most rational way to solve the problem of common defense. Pauses surrender European territory, not American; again, the United States has no effective answer—except to suggest that Europe is to be defended, and Europe will be the battlefield if war comes.

As the Atlantic alliance moves into the late 1960's, the United States has not modified its doctrines for the defense of Europe. In view of the political strains on European-American relations, how long can this approach—reflecting a strategic picture almost twenty years old—endure in the face of determined resistance from all the members of the alliance except its major advocate, the United States?

The American Theory of Alliance

Close to the previous analysis of the problems of defense has been another set of considerations: the American theory of alliance and the disparate images of this arrangement held by the European members of the Atlantic community. Again, doctrine and reality clash directly, and an understanding of the American position is essential to adequate comprehension of the tensions within NATO.

In American minds, NATO (and the North Atlantic Treaty upon which the organization is based) is the very model of the modern alliance system. American policymakers between 1947 and 1954 did their best to ring the Soviet Union with a set of politico-military arrangements designed to encompass all the Kremlin's neighbors; in these efforts, however, the image of the European alliance was predominant. All non-European alliances are as much like NATO as American ingenuity and leadership can make them.

When we generalize about "alliances," therefore, we are thinking particularly of NATO; observations about "allies" refer primarily to the European associates of the United States. We must allow for differences between European allies and those in Latin America and Asia, but in general the same principles apply. Our discussion of alliance in a European context can be regarded as basic to all American doctrine on the matter.

For the United States, alliances in the contemporary world are ways of organizing states under American leadership to defend a particular area against communist pressure. Their negative and restraining function, however, does not exhaust their usefulness. According to American theory, an anti-communist alliance also has a strategic mission in the larger conception of policy. An alliance, in other words, fits into an overall design and is expected to play a key role in many forms of American action beyond the deterrence of an armed communist attack.

Probably an alliance is most useful because it rationalizes and justifies the extension of American power and presence through commitments to a threatened area. In the early days of the Cold War, bogged down in the complexity of the problems facing the United States, Americans were less than unanimous about how to respond to them. One-shot policy declarations of opposition to further communist aggression, although obviously necessary, were inadequate. Alliances—backed by firm institutional structures—showed more concretely American interest and determination.

Thus, long before the appearance of the nuclear stalemate and the balance of terror, the United States was building a strategy of deterrence into its policy of alliances. NATO was the first overt implementation of strategic deterrence; the effect of the treaty and the military arrangements that followed served clear notice on the Soviet Union that any violation of the uneasy line between the two camps would immediately involve Moscow in a fight for its life. The Soviets might have been inclined to doubt a purely verbal American warning, but if Russian advances were impossible without inflicting American casualties, the message was unmistakable. The weaker and more vulnerable the area which the United States guaranteed, furthermore, the more critically important became the need to irrevocably commit American lives.

Except for the few Americans who dreamed of a new *pax Americana* enforced upon the whole world by American nuclear power, however, this military guarantee was no more than the beginning of a theory of alliance. The United States never intended permanently to carry the entire burden of defense of the NATO area; once American power had been thrown over Europe by word and deed, the states of the region must accept American assistance in organizing themselves and increasing their own capability for self-defense. "Self-help and mutual aid," words used by Secretary Marshall in the original presentation of the Marshall Plan in 1947, became a standard element in the American conception of alliance.

Actually, of course, the theory envisaged a continuum of development that began with weakness and the entry of American power, progressed through several stages of increasing defense capability, and culminated in local superiority over the communist forces across the line. In the early days this was known as creating "situations of strength." Framed originally and permanently in the NATO context, the notion of the build-up as the normal evolutionary pattern of an alliance became a firm tenet of American policy.

The transformation of a weak spot into a situation of

strength, as the United States sees it, requires several distinct steps. The first, it goes without saying, is the extension of American military and political protection over the region. Next is the establishment of U.S. political and military leadership, so that common policy can be determined. Then comes the problem of military and economic assistance to local allies to increase their capacity to resist aggression on their own and to contribute to the common effort.

Ideally, a region organized in this way is marked by political stability and economic viability common to all members, by intra-alliance harmony and unity of purpose, by programs of joint military or political action, by more or less elaborate institutions of consultation, policy-making, and joint action, and by a common front toward the Soviet Union and the non-aligned world on all important issues concerning the region. This is what American leaders have considered Elysium and toward which they have worked in NATO relations ever since the alliance was formed.

There is not the slightest doubt that American views of alliance—and especially of the Atlantic alliance—have been dominated from the outset by military evaluations and judgments. For a state to qualify as a "reliable ally" of the United States, the first requirement (and usually the key one) is that it accept the military and collective-defense implications of any alliance arrangements. This means that it must be willing to receive American military aid, American military advisers, and American military doctrine, and must also be content to fit the bulk of its own military program into an American-inspired plan. Its own military role is, in the last analysis, to be complementary to that of the United States.

In a political sense the United States demands one major commitment of its allies: a deep and articulate hostility to the Soviet Union, its allies and minions, Red China, and "international communism." Militant states, Americans argue, are more likely to cooperate in developing aid programs and joint plans than those with an equivocal attitude toward the Cold War. Ultimately, this "hard" attitude toward communism is the only requirement the United States imposes on internal allied politics. Other things being equal, Americans feel more comfortable allied with democratic regimes, but anti-communist authoritarians are to be preferred over uncertain democrats. In alliance relations, the ultimate test is pragmatic rather than ideological.

Clearly implied by American theory is that all problems within the alliance are to be met with a single and unified approach. Thus, a supramilitary dimension is added to the limited defense engagement of NATO; something resembling a bloc is expected to emerge from the close relationship of a treaty. An alliance is expected to do more than merely respond to a particular threat, or even to anticipate such a problem; hopefully, it will develop a positive approach, an integrated policy toward the many issues that arise in its region.

This leads again—by a different route, however—to the matter of the "common mission" and the need for intra-alliance "unity." The United States, finding in its NATO allies not only valuable military and political assistance but also the vital psychic satisfaction that comes from having friends in time of troubles, has been virtually obsessed with the desirability of maintaining at least the façade of NATO unity at almost any cost. In the process it has often given up opportunities for exploiting promising openings in other foreign policy areas, or at least has restricted its ability to move in other directions.

A standard case in point is the equivocal American position on anti-colonialism. Although the United States has generally supported the liquidation of the final remnants of imperialism, its record is nevertheless marked by a curious wavering. Since the major colonial powers were (and still are) NATO members, and since several of them were (and one or two of them still are) for understandable reasons reluctant to permit their colonies to go immediately to independence, they pressured Washington for support and were quick to invoke the symbolism of intra-alliance unity. It is obvious from the record that the American response was significantly affected, particularly in the matter of the Portuguese colonies.

The point is not that alliances are bad and anti-colonialism is good, but rather that an alliance is a special arrangement for a special purpose. Concern for its unity is appropriate only with regard to its own security questions. If NATO is an instrument for the defense of certain territories in Europe and North America, it is on these questions that unity is crucial. If anti-colonialism and its animosities minimize or reduce the effectiveness of the alliance in performing its function—a point not yet made persuasively with regard to any major ally—only then is there any real point in being agitated about unity.

The enervating effect of the American theory of alliance-unity-at-all-costs can be suggested in a more general context. In his famous speech at American University in June 1963, President Kennedy promised that the United States would make no deal with the Soviet Union "at the expense of other nations and other peoples, not merely because they are our partners but also because their interests and ours converge." This statement had a fine moral ring to it and reassured many of the President's listeners who were disturbed by certain other implications of this remarkable address. But for all its simple declaration of common intent, its clear thrust is that any and all deals are impossible.

What else is there for the United States to negotiate, after all, except questions on which its allies have claims and on which they express their own interests? The mark of an alliance leader is its willingness to consider and express the purposes of the alliance as a whole, not to serve as the instrument of wish-fulfillment of each and every one of its associates. It seems moderately remarkable that the badge of leadership worn by the United States so proudly is its voluntary grant of virtual veto power to so many of its smaller associates in relations with the communist world.

What makes the American fixation on intra-alliance unity so unrewarding is the way her European allies have treated the ideal. During the Suez crisis in 1956, the word "disarray" was used to characterize the state of NATO. Most American comment at the time (and ever since) was that "disarray" in NATO is dangerous and undesirable, and should be eliminated as soon as possible. But history suggests a different conclusion: disarray—that is, internal disagreement—has always been endemic in alliances. The United States, constantly seeking harmony and unity in the ranks of its associates, has instead been obliged to cope with an unending succession of crises.

To put it bluntly, the United States has been so preoccupied with maintaining at least the external appearance of NATO unity that it has often been forced to submit to a polite form of blackmail by enterprising and thick-skinned allies. European partners of the United States have been less addicted to this practice than some Asian and Latin American states, but even in NATO the technique is widely understood. American policy-makers have shown an unaccountable paralysis of will in the face of firm opposition from a major ally (including France, despite fiery protestations to the contrary by U.S. officials). As a result, the United States has been quick to offer compromises, or buy off the recalcitrant ally with reassurances or new commitments, or reverse itself completely. Appeasement is a vile epithet in the Cold War, but it has been a working principle (although never by that name) for many years in intra-alliance relations.

One issue on which the United States has never appeased is the future of Germany. Throughout the Cold War, Germany has been a central if not controlling element in America's European policy, much to the consternation of other NATO allies. As will be seen later, some European members of NATO are reluctant to embrace German good will as enthusiastically as the United States and are not convinced that resolution of the "German question" is the key to the solution of European-wide problems. But the United States has been unwilling to concede that its concern with Germany has been disproportionate in the larger picture of European problems; and the U.S. has virtually ignored the tensions thereby created, perhaps inhibiting the development of an effective partnership arrangement.

Even after a decade and a half of experience with NATO, it is still not clear why the United States is in any operational sense worried about alliance unity. Unless one assumes that either Europe or the United States has lost interest in protecting the West against communist attack, the original cement of the alliance is as firm as ever. Disagreements about issues outside NATO, even if they involve members of the alliance, should not be permitted to impair the performance of the central mission of the organization.

American cold-warriors devote considerable attention in their rhetoric to the possibility that the Soviet Union will somehow discover a method of "splitting the West." The elaborate rationale of unity has been constructed as a defense against this peril. But disagreement with the United States is not synonymous with rapprochement with Moscow—not, at least, since 1950—and to be continually palsied by the thought that some ally might, in defiance of both common sense and the experience of the entire Cold War period, be seduced by communist wiles at this late date would seem to be a reaction quite unworthy of a great power.

As in so much of contemporary American foreign policy, the American approach to NATO and to alliances in general reflects both the peculiarities of American history and the uncertainties of a young and relatively inexperienced power. NATO occupies its special place in American thinking partly because of the long-standing American bias about alliances in general and partly because to contemporary Americans an "ally" is also a "friend" and a source of real assurance.

Americans have insisted, from the moment of its birth, that NATO is not an "ordinary" alliance cut from the traditional cloth of nineteenth-century power politics. It is far more than that. The degree of institutionalization is unprecedented; nothing has ever been seen in interstate relations to rival the alliance's rich detail of planning and the proliferation of working committees, groups, councils, and conferences. Most revolutionary in American eyes is the major emphasis given to military integration.

This near idealization of NATO has made it all the more difficult for Americans generally to appreciate that European members of the organization regard it as "just another alliance." The arrangement has no intrinsic value to them but is relevant and worthwhile exactly to the extent that it advances their own notions of interest. Thus, Europe's demands for revision of the alliance are nothing more than routine readjustments of relationships, something inherent in good diplomacy, while to Americans they involve psychic issues of rejection, confession of past errors, and diminution of status.

This last point raises the second root of American attitudes toward NATO. The United States wants and needs allies to a major extent because it must have someone to lead, protect, and counsel. Nothing so reassures a people as being looked to for guidance by less fortunate nations— especially if the beneficiaries are appropriately grateful. A great power, Americans reason, must be a leader; to be a leader demands that there be followers. Followers in the natural course of events become allies; some may eventually become junior partners and enjoy a "special relationship," to wit, the United Kingdom since the early days of the Cold War.

This may appear to be a cruel judgment, yet the fervor and extreme language used today to re-create the nostalgic euphoria of the early days of NATO and to castigate the deviant behavior of General de Gaulle as a "traitor" and an "ingrate" suggest that Americans feel emotionally dependent on NATO to a surprising degree. Were the alliance to be destroyed, or even substantially modified to downgrade the American role, something important and irreplaceable might well go out of American policy. The consequences would be difficult to foretell, but they would certainly not be minor.

Where, then, does the American theory of alliance stand today? It seems clear that the United States expected too much of its allies and of the arrangement they made, while expecting too little of history. Americans, ignoring the onward march of events, have hoped that Europe would remain true to the political and military image the United States forged in 1949. Today an emotionally satisfying theory of the Atlantic alliance is at war with intractable facts.

The American Theory of Leadership

Because the role of the United States as leader of the Atlantic alliance and the entire free world is so firmly fixed in American minds, it has materially affected all important U.S. decisions about strategy and tactics vis-à-vis Europe since about 1948. It is central to a full-dimensional appreciation of American policy today. To put the issues in question form: What is the American theory of leadership? On what grounds does the United States claim primacy in its relations with its Western European associates?

The most obvious basis for the U.S. role is, of course, simple and uncomplicated power. The United States has such strength and freedom of action, compared with its allies, that no European state can seriously challenge its claim to first rank. But Americans, true to their tradition, can never be comfortable with considerations of "pure power." They feel impelled to discover some larger, more logical, and ultimately more moral foundation for U.S. primacy. The controlling theory of leadership thus grows out of an urge to rationalize and legalize the special power position of the United States.

American doctrine begins by reaffirming the self-evident: in any complex, closely knit organization, there must be real differentiation in status and role among the members. To accomplish its mission, an organization must have strong and dynamic leadership; leadership, to be effective, must have not only acquiescent followers but willing assistants, as well. Special qualifications are required both of leaders and of second-echelon chiefs; distinct traits are also, as a matter of fact, vital to good followers as well.

From this organizational premise the United States develops the components of its leadership role in the Atlantic alliance. In general, they add up to an American claim of superior insight into identifying problems, superior sagacity in devising policies, superior competence in making decisions, and superior dedication to the noble cause that unites the free world. No one would accuse the United States of being undeservedly modest in presenting its case to its allies and a candid world.

The United States has insisted from the very outset of

the Cold War that the true nature of the communist challenge was better understood in Washington than anywhere else in the world, and that the American interpretation of the menace should be controlling on the entire alliance, its members and its structure. Critics in Europe and elsewhere have pointed out that the United States was a relative late-comer in coping with communism, and that Europeans had been dealing with communist subversion and Soviet threats while Americans were insisting that the Soviet Union was a "noble experiment" and the Chinese communists were "agrarian reformers." This argument falls today—as it has always fallen—on deaf ears. The United States, with its global point of view and its commitment to high principles, can see the true dimension of communism in a uniquely clear light, and it would be a traitor to its own commitments if it permitted its allies to maintain erroneous judgments on so important a question.

American leadership extends also to the related problem of how best to meet the threat. Here a combination of prudential and rationalizing arguments is used to confer preeminence on American policy-making and decision-making. Since any allied actions to neutralize, deter, or turn back a Soviet challenge must involve a preponderant American role, the special place of the United States in determining what action should be taken has long been considered beyond dispute by all concerned. No alliance can count on effective joint action in the face of opposition from its most important member; American approval of alliance decisions therefore has been considered a *sine qua non* of European-American relations.

The argument, however, rests on other than these practical considerations. It must always be borne in mind that the American approach to contemporary Europe starts from the assumption that the Old World is a politically exhausted society, incapable of intelligently appraising situations or effectively dealing with them. Europe, almost by definition, cannot by itself (even less can any single European state) accurately evaluate the threat from the East, intelligently decide what to do about it, and vigorously and successfully prosecute a policy. Without the wise guidance and firm hand of the United States, Europe would stand as a helpless victim before Soviet aggression, susceptible either to systematic communist subversion or to obliteration by a single Soviet military strike.

Thus, in Cold War terms, the United States contends that its leadership role is essential to Europe's survival. But American responsibility for Europe's future goes beyond even the massive struggle with Moscow. The United States is quite convinced that it understands the long-term interests of Europe better than Europeans themselves do and is prepared to devote itself unstintingly to their fulfillment.

American comment on contemporary European policy often characterizes European attitudes as "provincial," always in contrast to the "international," "global," or "humanitarian" outlook of the United States. Today, Americans interpret Europe's revival and determination to pursue its own interests as retrogressive, "inward looking," and verging on isolationist. The United States is confident that American plans for world organization offer Europe a place much more in keeping with its true significance and unique genius.

Thus, the United States has more than once clashed directly with the states of Western Europe on precisely this issue of who is to be the custodian of European interests. The difficulties date from 1951 when the United States began insisting on levels and types of rearmament different from what Europe was interested in providing; after the defeat of the European Defense Community in 1954 came the Suez Crisis of 1956, the economic split in Europe after 1957 that culminated in British failure to join the Common

Market in 1963, and the contemporary squabble over nuclear weapons with France. In every case the United States has based its argument not on any sordid calculation of its own power interests, but rather on a genuinely disinterested advocacy of what was "best" for Europe. The only difficulty with this approach is that many—often most—Europeans simply do not agree with the American formulation of what is best for them.

American doctrines of leadership have been severely challenged in these divergences with Europe. The theory of the Cold War, the concept of the free world, and the idea of a common mission—all notions the United States has made its own—do not permit or prepare Americans to face real differences with their allies. When a crisis actually erupts, the first American reaction—at least among officials—is to deny its existence, to argue that "nothing fundamental has changed," and to paper over the quarrel with high-sounding but ominously empty communiqués. This evasive action normally is taken in the name of preserving alliance unity, a practice considered earlier in this chapter. Any newspaper reader today knows that ignoring such challenges to U.S. leadership, in the hope that they will quietly go away, has not worked very well.

When disagreement in Europe has been pushed to the point of open confrontation—as General de Gaulle has delighted in doing—the implications of American leadership have been made clear to Europe. In a real pinch, the United States insists that its own policies (even those determined unilaterally) are indistinguishable from alliance policy. This means that to oppose American formulas and enterprises is to injure the fabric of the Atlantic relationship, and any European government that does so must be prepared to suffer the consequences—which are formulated in Washington and presented to the other allies in hopes of forcing some form of censure on the recalcitrant government.

Here the discussion takes a decidedly ugly turn, both actually and potentially. When brought squarely to face this conclusion, cynical Europeans (frequently the French) inquire with some bitterness just what is the difference between being an ally of the United States and a satellite of the Soviet Union, and whether American "protection" is any more than a synonym for American "hegemony." The United States has never devised an effective riposte; by and large, Washington has invoked the common mission, the overriding threat from Moscow, and the gratitude of Europe for past American efforts to subdue the storm. But this is neither effective nor a reply.

United States leadership has had its greatest difficulty in denying (or, more accurately, attempting to deny) European states the right of autonomous judgment and decision on Cold War issues. Europeans insist, with considerable logic, that American interests and concerns with respect to the Soviet Union are considerably different from those of Europe. A major case in point is the concept of flexibility of response in defense; the United States is interested in keeping a minor war from becoming a major one, while Europeans are primarily concerned with keeping Soviet troops off free European soil. These two concerns, while closely related, are not identical. America is willing to sacrifice destruction and some European territory to gain the advantage of a pause, but Europeans reject the entire argument.

In these terms, it strikes Europeans as inconsistent when the United States demands that only the American approach to the Soviet Union will do. After all, announced American policy is to regularize Soviet-American relations as rapidly and extensively as possible (commensurate

with safety), and American statements repeat that no unilateral "deals" will be made with the Soviets at Europe's
expense. If American leadership demands that Europeans
subordinate their own initiatives toward Moscow while
Washington makes real progress toward relaxation, Europeans wonder about the advantages of having the United
States as the common spokesman.

This problem also shows up in issues not so clearly
involving the Soviet Union. For example, the entire movement toward economic and political integration of Europe
has, ever since its birth, had to deal directly with the question of the American role in Europe. It has never been
as tangled, furthermore, as it is today.

American support—official and public—of European integration springs originally from a Cold War root. An integrated Europe would be able to make a greater and
better-coordinated economic, political, and military contribution to the common cause of the free world. The United
States assumed as long ago as 1951, when the Schuman
Plan went into effect, that an integrated Europe would continue indefinitely to accept American leadership, and that
Europe's new gains would be placed behind the joint effort.

Not the least of the American reasons for favoring integration was that its realization would materially simplify
the task of leadership that Washington had so seriously
shouldered. To lead a single, well-organized, and enthusiastic integrated entity would be a much easier job than serving as chief of a collection of small but quarrelsome units.
America saw the improvement of Europe's position as a
plus factor in the world political situation, as an augmenta-
tion of the total strength of the free world—led, as always,
by the United States—in the struggle with Soviet aggression
and subversion.

In fact, American doctrine looked on the European effort to integrate as a joint enterprise of the entire Atlantic

bloc. The United States has lent financial support to the movement ever since 1951. After the success of the Common Market became obvious in Washington, the United States went even further and adopted the principle of supranationalism as the ideal organizing basis of an integrated Europe.

This immediately involved Americans in the bitter intra-European dispute between the "federalists" and the "nationalists"—an involvement all the more embarrassing because it was unnecessary. The case presented by the Brussels "Eurocrats," led by Jean Monnet, persuaded the United States, in large part because of its analogy with the American experience with federalism. But other theories of integration, which sacrificed some tightness of obligation in return for a broader range of membership and a more flexible approach to common problems, had considerable support in Europe as well. U.S. identification with the federalists has complicated the maintenance of an effective American position on the broader issue and has degraded the claims of U.S. leadership.

The severest test of American leadership, however, has come on the military issue of nuclear weapons. As part of its unique role in Europe, the United States has insisted that it preserve nuclear supremacy in the alliance. This has meant a concerted effort to reserve for itself a monopoly at least of nuclear decision and hopefully of command over all national nuclear forces. As part of this latter enterprise, Washington has always discouraged European efforts to establish national nuclear armories, excepting only the "special relationship" with its preferred European associate, Britain. This has challenged France's right and competence to develop its own set of weapons, and has set the stage for the contemporary showdown.

The American position on this problem is consistent with broader conceptions of the U.S. role that have been examined earlier; indeed, many of the doctrines of defense, alliance, and leadership that figure so largely in American self-justification converge exactly on the nuclear issue. Forcing the matter to an open test of strength, however, and raising doubts about the durability of the alliance unless the monopoly role of the United States is affirmed, does not seem to be the optimum way to establish a firm claim to leadership.

Both the question of European integration and the issue of nuclear weapons will receive closer attention later. They are mentioned here only to throw the issue of leadership by the United States into sharper perspective. They illustrate one of the major difficulties in the American approach to the leadership of Europe, a conceptual and operational failure that is plaguing the United States today and that will continue to exacerbate relations until it is corrected. This is the tendency of Americans to universalize their own concerns and to assume that the moral, legal, intellectual, and ethical pre-eminence of the American position on any question is so self-evident that all men of good will must automatically forsake all rival purposes.

What is the essential function of a leader in international affairs? The United States argues that a leader should point to the common goal, take major responsibility in bringing everyone to that goal, and call upon common resources in making the effort. There is, however, another theory that holds that the leader is the instrument of consensus, that he can act only on the basis of a clear and articulated agreement among the group, and that he is never allowed to go beyond the parameter of unanimity spelled out in advance. If the United States accepts the first theory, Europe today espouses the second.

Europe is perfectly willing to permit the United States to play the role of leader, provided that the common goal and the consensual procedures are well understood by all parties. American leadership toward ends to which Europeans subscribe is not only acceptable but quite welcome. American attempts to invoke the mystique of leadership to force (or to trick) Europeans into doing what they do not feel is in their individual and collective interests, however, has already shown its futility. Further attempts by Washington to use the strong hand will as clearly come to grief. A leader, after all, needs followers; one man does not make a parade. If leadership is indeed the American genius, it must be better suited to the problems it faces and the followers it seeks to enlist than it is today.

Chapter Four
The Reality, I:
Intra-European
Trends

So much, then, for the American image of postwar Europe and the doctrines upon which the United States has based its approach for the last two decades. What of the European reality? Where has the United States misread the course of events? What has happened during the past twenty years in Europe that the United States has overlooked?

A number of answers will be attempted in this chapter in an effort to pinpoint some of the major features of intra-European evolution that have not coincided with the American image of Europe and have therefore contributed to the contemporary impasse in transatlantic relations. The list will not be exhaustive, nor will the analysis of specific trends be the last word on the subject. The major claim here is more modest, yet perhaps more useful: in the aggregate, these elements have contributed largely to the shape of contemporary Europe, and a more effective U.S. policy must recognize them to a greater degree than at present.

Probably the most fundamental misapprehension that has bedeviled American policy springs naturally from the non-historic (or perhaps anti-historic) bias of so much of the American approach to foreign policy in general. American policy-makers have a sublime faith in precedent, enjoy nothing so much as to point out past failure as an excuse for not attempting new initiatives now, and see little reason to change existing policy—and none at all ever to admit having made such a change. But this reverence for past decisions (and past decision-makers) is not historic in outlook. History is characterized by dynamic evolution and change, not by stasis; a historical point of view accepts constant change as the norm of human experience and minimizes the effects of single cataclysmic reversals of relations.

All of this emphasizes the basic American misjudgment of the early postwar years. As the United States became acquainted with the condition of postwar Europe and the nature of its new responsibilities toward the Old World, Americans instinctively assumed that this "new normality" of a strong America and a weak Europe was a basic (and cataclysmic) reversal of roles, and that future history would be grounded on this relationship. Europe and America, each playing the new part in world affairs described in the preceding chapter, would remain (indefinitely, and therefore permanently) cast in their 1947 status and role. Implicit in this formulation, furthermore, was the basic assumption that changes in Europe would come about only as they were planned and executed by the United States.

This was really the source of the trouble in the first place, as it is indeed today. The United States will not—

perhaps cannot—come to terms with the stubborn historical fact that Europe since 1945 has returned to a truly self-determining force in world affairs. The "new normality" of 1947 is a historical curiosity today, and the status implications of the European-American relationship of the early Cold War are now shrugged off by Europeans as no longer meaningful.

A number of trends in Western Europe have contributed to the contemporary shape of the Old World. Each has had a perceptible influence on Europe's overall development, and each has, furthermore, been given special interpretive twists in American analysis.

The Political Renaissance of Europe

Probably the most powerful initial impression Americans received about Europe in 1947–1948 was one of political instability. The interwar era had been characterized by political—often revolutionary—change in many crucial areas of Europe; Germany and Italy had deliberately junked democracy for dictatorship; Spain had suffered a ruinous civil war; France had been all but ripped apart by corruption and scandal on the one hand, and abortive social revolution on the other; and Eastern Europe had throughout the 1920's and 1930's been a tinderbox of instability, ready to burst into flame at the slightest provocation.

During the 1930's, as war neared, the feebleness of European democracy was demonstrated repeatedly as both Britain and France proved unwilling and unable to resist the Nazi-fascist "wave of the future." Smaller democracies and free societies, like Czechoslovakia and Austria, were sacrificed to the Nazi appetite, while a hopeful republican government in Spain was snuffed out in a rebellion arrogantly subsidized by the dictators. By the time the Polish crisis ushered in a new era of open war, the cause of democracy in Europe had been debilitated to the point of danger.

The events of 1940 heightened the futility of free government. As Hitler swept across Europe and one democracy after another fell beneath the boots of the *Wehrmacht,* a dangerous elliptical conclusion began to take shape in important American minds, a concept that was to have important consequences a decade later: the only way to meet a strategy of dictatorial force is by a similar, but stronger, strategy of absolute counter-force. Democracy, the argument went, cannot withstand dictatorial pressure, nor can it mobilize adequate counter-pressure to turn back authoritarian initiatives. This rationale found its way into American Cold War rhetoric in later years as: "The only thing they (the Russians) understand is force."

In any case, Americans approached Europe after the war with a very low opinion of the survival value of democratic forces—with, of course, a few exceptions. Britain's stability and power were not only accepted but overestimated; in addition, the vitality of democracy was assumed in those small European states that had escaped the worst ravages of the war. Scandinavia, Switzerland, and Portugal seemed in relatively satisfactory condition. But elsewhere in Europe the political landscape was discouraging and unpromising in 1946–1947.

To begin with, the heart of Europe—Germany—was divided, occupied, and without any government at all. The two great continental members of the free coalition and would-be pillars of democracy, France and Italy, were rent by crisis because their governments could not make the simplest of decisions, and because powerful Communist parties in both countries were bent on sabotaging every effort at improvement. (Many Americans are surprised to be reminded that during this era there were communists in the cabinets of Italy and France.) The Low Countries were torn by the fallout of war: dynastic, religious, and linguistic quarrels. Austria was under occupation; Spain was still in the hands of a fascist dictator; the Balkans were heavily communist; and the general political scene—from the point of view of a partisan of democracy—was a very desolate one indeed.

As a result, the United States began its efforts to revitalize Western Europe believing that the growth of free government in Europe was bound to be slow, difficult, and perilous. Political instability on the continent was a norm of American planning. To this very day, Washington watches each political development in Europe for signs of renewed drift toward instability and crisis, and professes to be constantly concerned lest orderly political processes break down again. Scholars and officials in the United States are quick to advance reasons why existing European political arrangements cannot long endure on any reasonable basis; as a matter of fact, they often seem disappointed when their more dire predictions of political collapse fail to materialize.

No country has been more the victim of this pessimism than France. The general American approach to the political process in France since 1945 has been compounded of amusement, contempt, and dismay; French politics, admittedly incomprehensible to most Americans, tends always to receive a sinister interpretation in the United States. It is an item of faith among many Americans that "France cannot govern itself," and when—as under de Gaulle—the evidence of relative political efficiency is unmistakable, such success is credited to the fact that France has become a "dictatorship."

This assumption about the feebleness of Europe's political commitment and ability is largely responsible for the notion of American leadership in the Atlantic alliance. Behind all the American emphasis on European military weakness is always the conviction that Europe is politically incompetent to make valid judgments or decisions.

In fact, one of the most striking features of Europe's postwar history has been its political renaissance. There were serious political vacuums in many countries in 1945; fifteen years of depression, twelve years of Hitler, and six years of war had taken their inevitable toll. But political apathy and futility turned out to be transitory, and Europe and the Europeans proved to have a measure of political vitality that managed not only to keep countries, economies, and societies afloat through perilous times but even to make significant strides forward.

Probably the single most important element in the political rejuvenation of Western Europe has been the availability of leadership. Before the war, the democratic states of Europe had an unfortunate selection of leaders who were available to point the way through serious crisis. Daladier, Laval, and even Blum in France are names that do not enjoy lofty places in contemporary history; in Britain, Stanley Baldwin, Neville Chamberlain, and the other leaders of the 1930's have earned only a mixture of obloquy and pity as their reward from later generations.

Postwar Europe's leadership is interesting—and disquieting—in the extent to which it has been composed of men whose initial political impact was made before 1939. Even twenty years after V-E Day, important political figures in country after country in Europe were men who had come to maturity before the war and who held on to power in spite of their advancing years. The archetype was, of course, Konrad Adenauer in Germany, but Charles de Gaulle in France, Paul-Henri Spaak in Belgium, and others seemed to embody in their own personalities the anti-Hitler opposition of the 1930's.

This suggests one possible consequence of the interruption in political life that the Hitler era and the war brought about in many parts of Europe. Behind these older men, who sprang to positions of leadership in the confusion at the end of the Nazi years, there are today very few possible successors. Instead of a full pipe line of political figures who will, each in his turn, rise to prominence, in many European states today there is only the older group now holding power, then a rather large gap, and then a more or less undifferentiated mass of young political aspirants with limited experience but great ambition.

We see this factor at work, for example, in both West Germany and France. There are few middle-aged West German public figures; there are also relatively few middle-aged French politicians (at least very few in whom the French electorate has any confidence). Thus, Adenauer (and subsequently Erhard and others) and de Gaulle hold power while youthful and relatively undistinguished politicians mill around their Olympian figures. Only when an especially promising younger man—such as Franz-Josef Strauss in Bonn or Valery Giscard-d'Estaing in Paris—surfaces are any serious questions about succession asked. And even then, the simplest way to deal with the phenomenon of the bright young man who rises too soon is to remove him from the public eye.

Accordingly, judgments about Europe's political stability must usually be conditioned by considerations of leadership. West Germany seems to have weathered the storm of replacing Adenauer with Erhard; there will be some sort of crisis when Charles de Gaulle departs the scene. In Italy, the same tired politicians succeed each other in cabinet after cabinet. Of the other states, only in Britain does there seem to be any real hope that new leadership can regularly replace the old, the tired, and the careworn, or even the merely politically embarrassing predecessors.

When all is said and done, however, Western Europe's escape from the political collapse of the interwar years is a remarkable monument to the resiliency and tenacity of the old civilization. The largest share of the credit—at least initially—for the political rebirth of the continental states must go to the several political organizations of another ancient institution, the Roman Catholic Church. The forces of "Christian Democracy" that organized themselves into political parties in the immediate postwar period were more than anything else the modernized descendants of the old Center parties of prewar days. The Catholic parties were the first to move into the breach left by the repudiation of the prewar democratic parties and the elimination of the fascists. Christian Democracy squared off against communism in France and Italy, provided a fulcrum of power in West Germany and the Low Countries, and took power early in Italy, France, West Germany, and several smaller states. Only in France, furthermore, did the Catholic approach to politics fail to have a continued and useful life.

Although unabashedly Catholic in outlook, and although clearly looking to Rome for political, ideological, and organizational inspiration, Christian Democracy was and remains markedly left-wing in social viewpoint. This orientation is most obvious in the case of Italy's Christian Democratic party which gained a new lease on life late in the 1950's only by making a well-publicized "opening to the left," where new pools of consensus were to be found. In a larger sense, however, the leftward lean of Christian Democracy was in full harmony with an old tradition in the Church: the doctrine of "Christian social justice" identified with the encyclicals of Pope Leo XIII.

The success of the Catholic Church in returning effectively to politics brought another major political group quickly to the arena, a group that had been ruthlessly crushed during the Hitler era: the non-communist Left. Here the instrument of organization was usually the Socialist or Social Democratic party, found in virtually every Western European country except Spain and Portugal. The socialists were, and in many countries still are, torn between their firm commitment to orderly democratic procedures and their ideological insistence on rapid socio-economic reform. The first of these urges leads them to consider cooperation with the Christian Democrats; the second makes them at least sympathetic to the Communist parties. By and large, however, socialists in contemporary Europe today tend to minimize (and even seem to apologize for) their Marxist doctrines and to emphasize their belief in democratic government.

We can generalize very broadly about the course of Europe's political evolution since 1945. The first phase— a relatively short but extremely bitter one—consisted of a battle between nascent democratic parties and well-organized and militant communists. This struggle was concentrated in France and Italy, but there is little doubt that a communist victory in either country would have extended the conflict everywhere in Western Europe. Thanks to American intervention, however, indigenous Communist parties were beaten back and democracy gained (a sometimes perilous) control everywhere in liberated Europe.

With the communist issue more or less out of the way internally, the basic political drama of Europe has now been played out. In general, in most countries it has been a duel between socialists and non-socialists, with many national variations. In Germany the Social Democrats are the opposition; in Scandinavia a congeries of "bourgeois" (liberal, conservative, and agrarian) parties oppose a dominant Social Democrat majority; in Britain a two-party struggle between Labour (ostensibly socialist) and Conservatives controls politics; in the Low Countries socialism and Catholicism vie over small issues; in Italy Christian Democracy has made a working alliance with socialists in order to stave off a consistently powerful Communist party.

Only in France has the pattern been ruptured by the atypical phenomenon of Charles de Gaulle. Prior to his accession in 1958, France was also the scene of a Christian Democrat–Socialist interplay; the difficulty was that France's major problems, internal and external alike, were not being solved. De Gaulle's appeal is much like that of Jeanne d'Arc—suprapolitical—and in that sense he cannot be fitted into the common European pattern (indeed, he interrupts it in almost every sense, and this is perhaps his greatest source of strength). Closer analysis, however, indicates that the same social forces and groups that originally gave rise to France's version of Christian Democracy —the *Mouvement Républicain Populaire,* led by Georges Bidault in the immediate postwar period—today backs de Gaulle rather solidly, while it is the left (communist and non-communist alike) that opposes him. So we may perhaps tentatively place de Gaulle on the list of non-Left leaders in today's Europe, without drawing over-precise conclusions from such a classification.

Economic Recovery

A second major European trend important to the United States is economic recovery and a constantly escalating prosperity. The United States initially approached Europe when its political incompetence was matched by its economic prostration. Today Europe's political vitality is accompanied by a level of economic activity and a measure of personal well-being (with a few exceptions) unmatched in the continent's history.

Europe's economic recovery is a fact which American policy must obviously consider, but the prevailing American impression is that this high level of economic activity is basically unsound, susceptible to all sorts of pressures and difficulties, and liable to collapse on fairly short notice. A corollary often implied in this view, and on occasion expressed, is that Europe's prosperity is clearly the result of American programming in the early period (many Europeans would agree) and that its continuation depends upon the maintenance of close (and mutually profitable) ties with the United States.

A major factor in the difficulties that plague European-American relations today is the symbolism of economic independence as opposed to economic satellitism. Anti-Americans—especially Gaullists, but including a number of spokesmen from every European country—are quick to point to certain American investment and merchandising practices which look like attempts to make Europe a minor subsidiary. The ubiquity of a small number of trademarked American products, such as Coca-Cola and IBM, lends an unjustified credibility to this charge.

There is no doubt that American business has long cherished the European market and has sought—with some effect—to develop and maintain a privileged position there. As the European economy has developed and matured, furthermore, the interest of American corporations has shifted from mere marketing to large-scale investment and the creation of "wholly owned subsidiaries" operating entirely in Europe. A newly aggressive European entrepreneur could hardly be expected to welcome the active entry of American corporate giants into a relatively small economy in which he is just beginning to make headway. The combination myth-and-reality of an American economic takeover of Europe has produced major tensions.

Wrapped up in this private concern is one of public policy as well. The United States is vitally concerned with Europe's prosperity, with two qualifications. The first is that the United States may not want Europe to be prosperous enough to challenge successfully American economic supremacy in non-Western, European, or even American markets. A Europe fully developed and fully independent economically is no more valuable to American policy than one fully independent in political and military terms. A second qualification to American concern with European prosperity was hinted at earlier: American policy continues to insist that Europe's prosperity depends on American initiatives of all sorts, and that Europe should continue to acknowledge its dependence on the United States as part of the cost of maintaining the alliance.

This latter point will be examined in more detail later. Here we need only point out that in its basic thrust American policy expects—and on occasion demands—that Europe comport itself economically so as to meet American demands and needs. Failure on the part of Europe to play its appropriate role, furthermore, produces hurt feelings and accusations of selfishness and ingratitude.

But this is getting ahead of the story. The American point of view toward contemporary Europe's economic life was shaped, as was every other aspect of the image of Europe, during the early Cold War years. Americans remember Europe as it was in 1945, a ruin almost without hope, and recall that the United States had faith in Europe's capacity to recover when the Europeans themselves seemed to have lost their self-confidence and their belief in the future.

The Marshall Plan turned the economic tide in Europe by providing pump-priming capital in adequate amounts and appropriate forms. The first years after the war were an era of almost complete economic frustration: the United States poured in goods and money, but American assistance seemed to do no more than ward off starvation and total collapse. Not until the European Recovery Program was passed by the (Republican) 80th Congress did any sort of progress begin to be made toward economic recovery in Europe.

Three innovative features marked the Marshall Plan: first, it dealt with Europe as a planning unit rather than with the separate states; second, it emphasized "self-help and mutual aid" among Europeans as a prerequisite and concomitant to American assistance; third, it was programmed over four years, thus making possible the orderly rehabilitation of production and distribution facilities. These new directions in American assistance enabled Europe seriously to undertake recovery. Indeed, the Marshall Plan's effect upon European economic life was nothing less than electric.

Actually, recovery began even before American funds began to flow. In response to the American demand for "self-help and mutual aid," sixteen Western European states banded together into the Organization for European Economic Cooperation (OEEC); this was the body that led the way for intra-European economic cooperation and coordination during the Marshall Plan years, that outlined recovery plans for which American funds would be committed, and that provided the foundation on which subsequent integrative efforts would be based. OEEC remained in existence until 1960, when it was succeeded by the Organization for Economic Cooperation and Development (OECD), an American-inspired body designed to expedite the flow of Western capital into the developing areas of the world.

As soon as Europeans began concerting their efforts on

common economic problems, secure in the knowledge that the United States was behind them with aid, the European economic climate began to change dramatically. Production figures began to rise, new facilities were constructed, investment capital began to appear almost without warning, and recovery became almost a landslide. Never has money been better spent than were the $17-plus billion of Marshall Plan assistance, at least in terms of accomplishing the ends to which they were committed. In contemporary exchanges between Europe and America, one point is solidly on the American side: European prosperity does owe its start to American aid.

From the near-total economic prostration of 1947, the OEEC countries recovered so rapidly that generally by mid-1951 Western Europe had reached its prewar production level. This was only a statistical curiosity, however, for the upward curve of recovery swept by prewar figures without pause and kept rising almost without hesitation for another decade.

"Europe" had recovered magnificently, but not all parts of Europe recovered at the same rate or to the same extent. Germany's *Wirtschaftwunder* (economic miracle) is probably the best known of all the national recovery efforts, although Italy's force-fed industrialization did not lag far behind. Between 1947 and 1957, France, the Low Countries, and Scandinavia all passed through the most rapid phase of economic expansion they had ever known, even though they did not match the results produced by Ludwig Erhard or the Milan industrialists.

The slowest, most difficult, and least complete recovery was that of Great Britain. The consequences of Britain's inability to keep pace with its continental rivals and to play the special financial role that London traditionally has played—as well as steady abandonment of its world position—form a major part of Europe's contemporary dilemma. The fact that Britain has been, ever since 1945, the favored ally of the United States has complicated rather than simplified the problem, for Washington—in the interests of maintaining political solidarity—has consistently been willing to go the extra mile with London on economic matters. American policy has often extended concessions to Britain refused to other allies, and has acquiesced in British moves that would have been violently repudiated had they been undertaken by other European states.

This American-inspired "special relationship" with Britain has profoundly affected Washington's support of continental economic (and hopefully political) integration. Britain, more closely tied to the United States than the other nations of Western Europe, has attempted to maintain its historic position of insularity vis-à-vis the continent, with the result that it has been on the outside looking in at most integration schemes. This, in turn, has further complicated United States policy encouraging European unification.

In economic terms, European integration has focused successively on production and then upon trade. Production was first approached during the period of Marshall Plan aid, when the European Coal and Steel Community was created in 1951 in accordance with the provisions of the "Schuman Plan." Here for the first time appeared the "Six," the core states of continental Western Europe, whose willingness to merge their economic destinies has played so large a part in creating the Europe of today: France, West Germany, Italy, Belgium, the Netherlands, and Luxemburg.

The effect of ECSC was to eliminate all national frontiers in the production of coal, iron, and steel. Producers no longer needed to be concerned with national origins of the coking coal, the iron ore, or the scrap that went into the steel they made—nor did they have to deal with national inhibitions in marketing their products. This simple but revolutionary idea—that economic needs took precedence over national identities—has permeated European economic thinking ever since.

Six years after the experience of the Coal and Steel Community had proved that production could be usefully and profitably integrated in such a key commodity as steel, the same six nations took an even more far-reaching step: they negotiated the 1957 Treaty of Rome that inaugurated the European Economic Community, the "Common Market" that was pledged to the elimination of all tariff barriers among its members within a twelve-year period. Although beset by nationalism and the pursuit of particular advantage by some member governments, the EEC in a few years has gone even further than the ECSC to rearrange economic lines among the Six.

From the U.S. point of view, perhaps the most important element in the economic integration of Western Europe is that Great Britain has never been a participant. London was given a chance to come into both the Schuman Plan (ECSC) and the Monnet Plan (EEC) at the beginning, but in both cases it found adequate reason to refuse to merge its economic life with the states of the continent. Inevitably, Britain fell behind Europe's overall growth rate, and most markedly (and embarrassingly) fell significantly behind the Six.

London's initial reply to the economic threat from the continent was to establish its own trading bloc on the mainland in the form of the European Free Trade Association (EFTA, formed in 1959). EFTA included Britain, Denmark, Norway, Sweden, Switzerland, Austria, and Portugal: a rather ill-assorted group with no firm pattern of reciprocal trade except in the case of Britain and Scandinavia, and no trade lines representing the major interests of any power except Britain itself. EFTA became known in American and British circles as the "Seven," an offset to the "Six."

What Britain hoped to accomplish by EFTA was fairly clear. By denying the EEC its most obvious and promising new recruits, London hoped to inhibit the Common Market's growth. Britain also hoped to develop EFTA to the point where it could bargain collectively with the EEC on a merger of the two organizations. In its trade-bloc maneuvering, furthermore, London was never obstructed by Washington—even though the United States by 1958 had committed itself to the EEC's theory of integration and was therefore concerned over the rapidly growing split in Europe. The pull of Britain on American policy, however, was and is still so powerful that Washington could not bring itself to put any pressure on London to take the route of the EEC.

Finally, in 1962 Britain took the irrevocable step and applied for admission to the EEC as an individual state and not as the leader of a rival trade bloc. Several of its fellow EFTA members also made applications, each contingent on Britain's entry. Negotiations were long and tortuous, but in January 1963, in one of the major political decisions of the postwar era, de Gaulle's France vetoed British entry on the ground that the United Kingdom was not "European enough." This was a political, not an economic, judgment; what the French President was saying in effect was that Britain was too dependent—militarily, politically, and psychologically—on the United States and could not be a loyal member of an exclusively European club.

One moral, however, is pointed out by the controversy over integration: the prize is important enough to be worth the quarrel. This underscores the point that Europe's economic vitality is well based and that Western Europe is now an economic entity of great power and strength. The

United States need no longer regard Western Europe as in any sense its economic pensioner, dependent on American policy for the direction of its evolution. There is adequate economic capacity in Europe to make it possible for the states of the region to shape their own economic destinies, either individually or in concert. Europe's economic revival is complete.

Integration: Theory and Reality

Western Europe was the birthplace of the modern nation-state and the political creed of nationalism. The doctrine first gained mass acceptance in revolutionary France—that each individual formed a part of a larger whole, the nation, to which he owed allegiance, service, and perhaps even his life. Modern international politics is founded on the institution of the nation-state, and the interplay of national groups, organized into states and operating through governments, forms the content of the business of diplomacy and war.

It was as a group of nation-states that Western Europe acquired its dominant place in world affairs. Scholars speak of the "universalization of the European system" in the nineteenth century; what they mean is simply that after the close of the Napoleonic wars, the European system of states-and-nations, occupying itself with what was advertised as a normal and creditable enterprise—imperialism—extended its domain and its institutions everywhere in the world. By 1900 European methods of conducting political business were spread widely—if unevenly—around the globe.

In one sense, the Western—that is, the European—state system has reaped since 1945 the consequences of its nineteenth-century success. The concepts of politics, of which nationalism and the sacred character of the nation-state are central, have taken firm root in the non-Western world, and Europeans have seen their overseas empires disappear under an avalanche of slogans which Europe itself spawned a century or more ago.

At a time when so much of the world is intoxicated with nationalist separatism, it is significant that in Western Europe—where it all started—one of the most important evolutionary trends has run in exactly the opposite direction. What we have called "integration" is many things, but no matter in what guise it appears, the integrative process retains one central characteristic: it attacks head-on the basic premises of nationalist separatism and argues the superior values of supranational cooperation.

Western Europe has been the scene of the most impressive assault on the principle of national sovereignty since the state system was born. The struggle between supranationalism and nationalism has been going on there for two decades, and the final outcome remains inconclusive today. But the fact that supranational and integrative influences that reach beyond such ancient units as "Germany" or "France" continue to battle and to win limited but real victories in important areas suggests that the impact of integration on Western Europe will be a permanent one.

Probably the major mistake made by outsiders—particularly Americans—in evaluating the significance of the trend toward integration has been to judge it largely in terms of its institutional products. Because economic institutions have had considerable success while political and military ones have proved impossible to create, many analysts contend that integration is primarily an economic phenomenon. Nothing could be further from the truth.

Integration is fundamentally and permanently not economic, or political, or prudential, but rather psychic and emotional. In other words, no integrative institutions could be created or joint enterprises undertaken without a willingness among the people affected. Thus, supranationalism really involves a crisis of loyalty.

The nation-state has, for at least 175 years, brooked no rivals as the vehicle of ultimate loyalty for the individual. For any supranational institution to function effectively requires some erosion of loyalty to the nation-state, some generalized awareness that one's loyalty and one's interests lie in a broader community. A crisis can help disperse such an appreciation throughout a population, and World War II and its aftermath provided exactly this spur to self-realization in Western Europe.

The war made it crystal clear that the states of Europe were no longer efficient political organizations; Europe could tear itself apart, but it could not solve its own problems so long as it acted through historical state forms. The helplessness of Europe in the face of Soviet and American power in the postwar period underscored the point. If there was any value in the European way of doing things that was worth saving, Europeans could protect that value only by acting and thinking in terms of "Europe" as a culture complex and an action unit.

This was the role played by the "European Movement" in the immediate postwar years. Leaders from all the states of free Europe—including Winston Churchill, Count Carlo Sforza of Italy, Paul-Henri Spaak of Belgium, Robert Schuman of France, and many others—formed a voluntary organization of agitation and propaganda during Western Europe's darkest era. Their message was simple: to save itself, Europe must unite. The group made no serious attempt to devise solutions to Europe's problems, but this was really not its purpose. Between 1945 and 1950 the European Movement (that reached something of a climax in the creation of the Council of Europe in 1949) kept alive the notion of supranationalism as the way to salvation.

The Schuman Plan of 1951 was the first real fruit of supranationalism in Europe, and its success emboldened the integrationists. At this point they made a near-fatal error; having broken through the façade of sovereignty at an important point—the production of steel—they apparently thought they could go through at virtually any other point as well. The failure of the project for a "European Army" in 1954, under the European Defense Community, taught them that loyalty is transferred a little at a time. What people will accept in one area may be too much for them in another.

Accordingly, the rapid politicalization of the trend toward integration that some of the more enthusiastic "Europeans" had in mind was abandoned and replaced by a deliberate return to "functionalism." The entire spectrum of governmental action was surveyed in search of a "soft spot" that would yield to fairly rapid action. Two such spots were found in the mid-1950's: intra-European trade and the development of nuclear energy.

Treaties among the "Six" quickly created the European Economic Community and the European Atomic Energy Community (EURATOM). Together with the Coal and Steel Community that had been in business for half a dozen years, the three functional bodies became the "European Community" and developed some of the characteristics of an established order. The Community has a capital, Brussels; it has functionaries who are simultaneously missionaries and technicians, and who are known informally as "Eurocrats"; it has its symbolic leaders, among whom Jean Monnet of France stands pre-eminent, with Sicco Mansholt of the Netherlands and Walter Hallstein of West Germany close behind.

For reasons we have briefly considered earlier, the United States came to be an enthusiastic sponsor of supranational integration. More than anything else, Washington saw an integrated Europe as a "stronger" ally, better organized to make its contribution to the common effort against communism. History and logic combined to make the process of European federation—involving the transfer of sovereignty from national units to some new central body—a concept relatively simple for Americans to understand, for it was so analogous to the American experience. As a result, by the time the Kennedy administration took office in 1961 the United States had committed itself completely to the Brussels approach to integration, and had found in Jean Monnet the most authentic voice of the new Europe.

Here again the American vice of oversimplification led the United States astray. Washington contended—indeed, contends today—that a true "European" must be a supranationalist and a federalist. Any trafficking with the Gaullist concept of a "Europe of states," in which national sovereignty is retained, brands one a hopeless reactionary and at heart an opponent of European progress and prosperity. The United States has learned painfully that it is possible to be a "good European" while retaining some serious reservations about the Common Market or the political unification of the continent.

Charles de Gaulle has been most directly identified with the anti-federalist approach to Europe, and his opposition to the Brussels approach is one of the major entries in the bill of particulars the United States has been drawing up against him. But he is by no means alone. It is not at all certain that West Germany, or Great Britain, or even Italy would enthusiastically forfeit major elements of sovereignty to an untried central authority—at least at the present level of institutional development. Federation tends to be the most desirable approach for the smaller countries, and today it is the Benelux complex that sees the greatest advantage to it.

We shall examine the French position in greater detail

in a later chapter. Here let us only point out that the French contend they are interested less in institutional change than they are with the beneficial results of cooperative action. If, de Gaulle argues, concern with the principle of federation impairs progress toward concrete goals of integration, then neither side of the argument is satisfied. On the other hand, continued progress toward joint (or common) policy, using existing state forms, will produce useful results while leaving open the question of the eventual institutional structure of Europe. France thus strikes a pragmatic note while criticizing its adversaries as zealots and ideologues.

The argument between the federalists and the defenders of sovereignty will probably not be settled in this generation. A final verdict may await the inexorable processes of history or may come about as the result of a more sudden turn of events. One simple factor may well be of major importance in the years ahead: the chronological one. By and large, in most of the countries of the continent, federalists are younger than nationalists by a considerable margin.

The crucial age seems to be about thirty-five. There are many federalists above this age, of course; but in general, nationalists are more common. Furthermore, it seems, the older the age group, the more pronounced its bias against federalism for Europe. Conversely, the younger the age group, the stronger and deeper seems to be its commitment to federation and a tightly integrated Europe.

If this age cleavage is correct, there is a strong temptation to infer that time will gradually usher in the federalists as the older nationalists exit and leave the stage free. Certainly some of the more outspoken young leaders in Western Europe today express this opinion; to listen to them, it seems that only the removal of a small group of stubborn old men stands between the present and the achievement of federation.

This seems somewhat too simple a forecast. The nation-states of Europe no longer hold the total loyalty of their people, but they are far from being replaced soon by an integrated federal structure. The next generation of Europe's leaders will be, as we have pointed out, much younger than the contemporary crop. This will have a perceptible effect on national politics and progress toward integration, but it will not of itself open the door to quick and early federation.

What the argument over federalism has done, however, is to make the federal alternative a conceivable course of action for Europe. Through existing institutions and the continuing debate between the Gaullists and Eurocrats, the politically articulate segment of European society knows that it has a choice to make some time in the future. "Europe" as a working concept and as a vehicle for some sort of loyalty has already won acceptance; the contemporary discussion centers on how best to bring the idea of "Europeness" to fruition.

It seems quite clear, also, that this is a question only Europeans can answer, and that outside interference will almost certainly create problems. "Outside" in this context means, of course, the United States, but it also means (or, at least, has meant up to the present) Great Britain. Rightly or wrongly, large segments of continental opinion are convinced that Britain has been playing its traditional role of trying to divide and balance the continental powers, and that London fears European integration. President de Gaulle's castigation of Britain as "not European" was well understood—if not universally accepted—everywhere on the continent.

Were London to make a massive reappraisal and finally cast its lot with Europe—even at the expense of its American and Commonwealth ties—a completely different situation would come about. The federation versus nation-state debate would doubtless be intensified, but with a much greater overtone of realism. Europe with Britain would be able to solve its organizational problems relatively simply because its potential for action would be so great.

The Rebirth of Nationalism

Curiously, running alongside the trend toward integration, especially in the 1960's, has been the opposite trend: what we may call the rebirth of European nationalism. Indicative of this trend has been the threatened revival of Nazi-type nationalism in Germany, continued British reluctance to participate in the Communities of the Six, and, of more concern to the United States, the continued insistence by Charles de Gaulle of French independence of action, irrespective of prior commitments to the organizations of Western Europe. Characteristic of the latter is a statement made by French Foreign Minister Michel Debré at Metz in October 1960: "In Europe, legitimate power is the power which comes from national sovereignty, and against this power arbitrary outside tyrannies like the so-called 'supranational' institutions can do nothing."

In most continental states nationalism was an early casualty of the postwar years. At a time when traditional states had demonstrated their inability to prevent near destruction and total ruin in a highly civilized portion of the world, at a moment when beliefs of all sorts had been virtually exhausted by years of unending struggle for simple survival, it was not surprising that pleas for nationalism fell on deaf ears. Indeed, this semi-collapse of nationalism allowed integrationists to gain their initial hearing.

It was, for example, remarkable that the great projects for supranational organization were all initiated by Frenchmen, citizens of the state that had invented nationalism and that had for so long symbolized the collective search for prestige, glory, and leadership in world affairs. The first great integrative move was the Schuman Plan, put forth by Robert Schuman, then Premier of France. The European Defense Community was the brainchild of René Pléven, then French Minister of Defense. And the European Economic Community, as we have noted, was more than anything else the creation of Jean Monnet, who as Finance Minister in successive Fourth Republic governments had come to sense the problems of trade and development.

What is more, not only did France produce the three great projects for integration; it accepted two of them. But the EDC's failure in 1954 was a warning; although tied up with the complex maneuvers of Premier Mendes-France with regard to Algeria and Indochina, in the last analysis it was a flare-up of nationalist bias against *"le boche"* that brought the project to grief. Even so, however, for France to go so far in the direction of supranationalism was a significant event.

In Germany twelve years of Hitler had reduced nationalism to an obscene travesty. The Nazis had systematically destroyed or converted every competing vehicle of loyalty and left the German people with only their membership in the nation (the Nazi *"Volk"*) to sustain them. When the Nazi regime collapsed, it left millions of Germans with nothing at all to belong to, nothing to identify with. Furthermore, there was widespread suspicion in West Germany that extraordinary efforts would have to be made before Germany and the Germans would be readmitted to the circle of respectable and respected peoples. Thus, integration met basic German needs: it provided a focus at a time when one was badly needed, and it involved Germans in cooperative enterprises with other Europeans and helped to overcome some of the more extreme forms of anti-German bias.

The political history of the Federal Republic of Germany

raises another interesting point. Many—perhaps most—of the political leaders in West Germany today fear a revival of German nationalism and go to considerable lengths to keep any tendencies in that direction under control. It would appear that Germans have learned from their recent history one very powerful lesson: nationalism is too potentially dangerous a force on the German personality to be allowed free play.

On the other hand, clever German politicians have not been above using the specter of a possible revival of Nazi-type nationalism as a weapon of foreign policy, particularly in dealing with the United States. As we shall see later, in the nuclear debates of recent years, German spokesmen have alluded to the possibility of undesirable consequences if Germans are denied their legitimate aspirations. How real and serious these dangers are, no one can estimate; but even the possibilities have made the United States reluctant to disappoint Germany in many situations.

In Italy, in spite of more than two decades of fascist rule, nationalism never took really solid root. Under Mussolini, Italians seemed to have enjoyed the show without ever taking it seriously; it is interesting that Italy's first postwar constitution called for Italian adherence to any future federal political arrangements that might be established either in Europe or on some wider basis.

Of the larger states of Western Europe, Italy has remained most untouched by the renaissance of nationalism that has so clearly marked the early 1960's. Perhaps because Italians retain even today their traditional skepticism and cynical approach to politics, they have remained immune to the temptation to discover peculiar values and sacrosanct virtues in their national group. Italy's approach to integration has been a highly pragmatic one, but its commitment to the idea has been more lasting than that of some other countries.

Great Britain, once again, is an exception to the trend toward integration in the postwar decade. The British survived the war more convinced than ever that they were not "merely" Europeans but were of some other and more worthy clay; they were also the only people in Europe who could argue seriously that their country was a "victor" in the war. As a result—in spite of Winston Churchill's early participation in the European Movement—Britain from 1945 onward tended to view the continent as something apart, interesting but outside British involvement.

Britain's refusal to participate in either the Coal and Steel Community or the Common Market—although invited to do so in both cases—was to some extent based on reasonable economic and political grounds, but in the last analysis it was the inevitable result of Britain's non-identification with the European states that are its neighbors and allies. Britons of all levels of association and sophistication found it unacceptable to merge their destiny with that of the "Europeans," and sought instead a unique position more in keeping with the United Kingdom's traditional "splendid isolation" from the affairs of the mainland and with its "special relationship" with the United States.

As we shall see later, Britain is paying today for this nineteenth-century hangover. Britain is slowly and painfully reconciling itself to discovering its new future as only a part —but by no means an unimportant part—of a "Europe" from which it has been aloof for three centuries.

But the nationalism that is most evident in contemporary Europe, that disturbs the United States and American policy the most, and that may turn out to be dangerously contagious, is that of Charles de Gaulle's France. Indeed, the change in the political climate of France—and therefore of all Western Europe—since the return of the general to power in 1958 is one of the most important elements in the entire postwar history of Europe. Under the Fourth Republic the French were agonizingly aware of their inability to solve either foreign or domestic problems. Their pride and self-respect—what the French call *amour propre*—was not dead but muted by circumstances. Since de Gaulle, however, the French political outlook is entirely different.

Most noticeably, the general has been able to play the role of Jeanne d'Arc and to reinvigorate French patriotism. He has been able to tap the powerful springs of emotion that Frenchmen traditionally pour forth for *la patrie*. He has made his people again proud to be French and eager to show (if not flaunt) French uniqueness and special excellence to the world.

This insistence upon making a French presence felt in European situations and increasingly in the world at large has led de Gaulle and his government into direct conflict with the United States. He is not a latter-day spokesman of the court of Napoleon (nor is he a new Louis XIV or Napoleon himself, as certain disgruntled American policy-makers are fond of calling him); he is a patriotic Frenchman, leading a nation of equally patriotic citizens, who start from a premise they find self-evident—and which the United States rejects as intrinsically unsound. This is no less than the equality of French prestige, French honor, French policy, and French judgment with those of any other country, including the United States.

This is nationalism, pure and simple. It has led de Gaulle's France into unwise and extreme positions in dealing with the Common Market, positions far more militant than French public opinion would tolerate. The 1965 elections in France clearly pointed out that the Gaullists had gone a bit too far, and the speed with which Paris reestablished a *modus vivendi* with the Eurocrats in Brussels testifies to the inherent elasticity of de Gaulle's regime. But it has also led de Gaulle into rejecting the "integrated command" aspects of NATO on the grounds that in time of peace

French troops may not be commanded by non-Frenchmen, and non-French forces may not be stationed on French soil —again, concepts drawing upon the most basic of nationalist urges.

There is little reason to suspect, however, that France's anti-NATO position will prove as unpopular as did the Common Market stance. We shall examine the NATO issue in detail later; for the moment, we shall say only that French "independence" from American "hegemony" and France's "equality" in dealing with the United States are long-standing positions originally voiced by successive leaders under the Fourth Republic. De Gaulle's strictures against the American posture in NATO, furthermore, are not his alone; at a lower level of verbalization, and probably at a lower level of commitment as well, they are rather widely shared among the European allies.

So the example of France, which found in a time of prosperity and relative security a worth in nationalism it could not discover in time of collapse and disorganization, may well be emulated by other states in Europe. It is too much to say, as some cynical Americans allege, that integration is a spent force and that nineteenth-century nationalism is the order of the day in Europe. Such complaints usually turn out to be preludes to denunciations of de Gaulle with no useful purpose. But nationalism is a force today, coexisting more or less comfortably with supranationalism in all the states of Europe and frequently within the spirit of individual Europeans. American policy must carefully take account of the nationalist-integrationist confrontation and calculate its effects for decades to come.

The Erosion of the Iron Curtain

One more development in Europe has passed almost unnoticed but is of major portent: the erosion of the Iron Curtain. Although never as complete as the United States thought it was and wished it to be, the division of Europe has been breaking down steadily for the past decade. Today, as far as Europeans are concerned, it plays an obstructing but peripheral role in the evolution of the new Europe.

Two major forces have contributed to this erosion of the barrier. The first is economics. Neither extensive Soviet efforts to reorient the economic relations of its satellites toward itself, nor American insistence on various forms of boycott and trade restrictions, has succeeded over the long haul in invalidating the natural and complementary economic relationship between Western and Eastern Europe. East-West trade was never completely halted, even at the highest pitch of the Cold War; as the militancy of the Soviet-American confrontation has relaxed, economic relations have steadily increased between Eastern European states seeking goods unobtainable from communist sources and Western European states hungry for markets.

Today, with the satellites in all but open economic revolt against Soviet domination, and with the states of Western Europe selling to (and buying from) Eastern Europe (and the Soviet Union) with complete freedom, the economic division of Europe is almost completely a thing of the past. Certainly on the communist side great obstacles remain, as the Soviet Union gives ground to its satellites only reluctantly. On the Western side of the Iron Curtain a few political inhibitions remain, but they are rapidly dissolving. The future—barring a major political crisis—seems clear: a steady increase in economic intercourse as economies on both sides of the Iron Curtain continue to grow.

The second factor that has gone far to vitiate the division of Europe has been the rise of Europe-wide youth movements. It was through *rapprochement* between youth groups in both West and East that the Iron Curtain began systematically and extensively to be breached. (We scarcely need to point out here that the youth groups we are discussing are not the communist-inspired "youth festivals" in various Eastern European capitals.) The essence of the meeting of youth in today's Europe is that it is determinedly non-ideological and based on a pursuit of common interests. European young people are highly organized, with almost every interest and line of activity having its own supranational or international organization which holds congresses, meetings, or other gatherings regularly. Politically articulate youths in most of the countries of the West, including generally the future political elites of their respective societies, now boast international circles of friends and a sense of shared purpose which will obviously have a major effect when they ascend to the seats of power.

Yet youth movements and economics cannot be given all the credit for the erosion of the Iron Curtain. It is a simple fact that for millions of Europeans the political division of Europe into Soviet and American spheres of influence was completely unnatural and an artificial consequence of the war—something to be eliminated as soon as possible. The highly expedient division of Germany only symbolized the problem.

Europeans admit today that the most brutal remnant of the Curtain, the barrier that still divides the German nation, will be the last to fall; nevertheless, considerable economic, cultural, and personal relations go on between the two Germanies (excepting only the two Berlins). Elsewhere, the notion of unity for all Europe gains more adherents as the Cold War retreats, and prospects for "reunification" of the whole continent grow brighter.

Again, we must turn to Charles de Gaulle. His idea of a Europe "from the Atlantic to the Urals" strikes a chill in the hearts of most American cold warriors, for it raises the prospect of a working arrangement between Western Europe and the Soviet Union. But the notion has many adherents in Europe, East and West—although without much clear understanding of its political implications. For most Europeans—and possibly for de Gaulle himself—the phrase connotes the point that we have been making here: Europe is a unity, at least culturally and perhaps economically, and the boundary line of Europe runs far enough to the East to include European Russia. Whether a sinister political maneuver or merely the expression of a more or less pious hope for a better future, "from the Atlantic to the Urals" is a notion of major relevance in the future of all-European evolution, and therefore one which the United States must consider carefully.

Chapter Five
The Reality, II:
Atlantic Relations

One of the most striking examples of the discontinuity between image and reality, of which we have already said so much, is the nature of Atlantic relationships during the postwar period. Most Americans, fed a steady diet of pro-NATO rhetoric from official and Establishment sources for the past decade and a half, view the history of postwar European-American relations as one of almost unbroken amity and cooperation, at least until very recently when evil influences emanating from Paris have fouled what had been a beautiful relationship. The image is so enchanting, the relationship so idyllic that one hates to contradict the dream with uncomfortable reality. Yet the truth of Atlantic relations since 1945 bears little resemblance to the American image.

It is true, of course, that the Marshall Plan was warmly welcomed in Europe, and that during the four years from fiscal 1948 to fiscal 1952 Europe rang with praise of American generosity, American wisdom, and American courage. Looking back on that era, we may wonder how normally cynical Americans, private and official, allowed themselves to be taken in so easily. It was natural for Europeans to praise the United States during the term of Marshall Plan aid; after all, the U.S. was making it possible for Europe to do what it wanted very badly to do anyway and was demanding no immediate repayment other than loud gratitude. It was a very favorable bargain for Europe, and the governments were free with laudatory comments on American action.

Negotiation of the North Atlantic Treaty, beginning late in 1948, was not so universally welcomed, however. The United States was still, by any account, making a generous offer of protection, but implicit in the project were some new demands by Washington. "Self-help and mutual aid" meant one thing when applied to economic recovery in Europe, but tended to mean something quite different in a context of European defense. Several eager Marshall Plan participants proved much more reluctant to join the Atlantic Pact.

Even so, however, as long as the Marshall Plan continued to set the pattern of American policy in Europe, the climate of relations continued warm, and American attitudes became fixed. The United States concluded that Atlantic relations were "normal" and "stable" only when Washington was playing an expansive role before an audience of loudly admiring and appreciative junior associates. U.S. activism, European gratitude and cooperation—this was the optimum relationship.

The End of Euphoria: 1951–1952

It is possible to pinpoint rather accurately the moment when the euphoria of the Marshall Plan began to give way rapidly to disagreement and conflict in European-American relations. It was the day the United States Congress enacted the Mutual Security Act of 1951 and changed the dynamic of American policy from a context of economic aid to one of common defense. From that time forward— that is, during the entire history of NATO as an organization—there have been powerful cross-purposes at work in allied relations and growing cleavages within the coalition as a whole.

From the American point of view, the Mutual Security Act was simple good sense. Europe had recovered economically, and by 1951 European prosperity had come to be viewed as a contribution to the free-world effort to contain communism. It was, therefore, only just and fair that the newly solvent and stable states of Western Europe do their bit for the common defense. In addition to limiting further aid to Europe to direct military-security areas, the United States made it clear to its allies that the time had come to abandon their overriding concern with recovery and their new prosperity, and instead to initiate major programs of rearmament.

Apparently to the complete astonishment of the American government, most of the European allies objected strenuously. They saw no reason to risk the stability of their governments by telling their people that it was necessary to lower their painfully raised standard of living in order to re-create military machines, at least so soon after the end of the war. It was at this moment that France first appeared as the most outspoken opponent of American policy, a role it was to play consistently thereafter.

The United States would not yield, however, and instead pushed ahead with the creation of the North Atlantic Treaty Organization (NATO, we must always remember in spite of journalistic carelessness to the contrary, stands for the *organization* that was created at the Lisbon meeting of the North Atlantic Council in 1951, and not for the *treaty* that dates from 1949) and the development of extensive plans for the defense of Europe against Soviet attack. Washington preferred not to hear the murmuring from France, Scandinavia, the Low Countries, and even from some British quarters that the United States was moving too rapidly to fit the Western position in Europe into a military mold.

France, as a matter of fact, questioned the necessity of any NATO at all. It was generally accepted in Western Europe—and in many American circles as well—that the North Atlantic Treaty of 1949 was inspired by and a reply to the Czech and Hungarian coups of 1948. By throwing American protection over Western Europe, the United States was unmistakably warning the Soviet Union not to carry its technique of the coup—the "inside job"—any farther west. In the French view, once the treaty was negotiated its effectiveness was complete, and additional institutionalization would serve no useful purpose. The French, however, are realists; seeing that the United States was determined to have NATO, France went along. As events were shortly to demonstrate—long before Charles de Gaulle re-emerged from Colombey-les-Deux-Eglises—the French went into NATO deliberately to extract every potential advantage while accepting as few inhibitions as possible on their own freedom of action—and those few only under loud protest.

Washington saw the creation of NATO as a landmark of

Atlantic policy, and there were a few voices in Europe that shared the American point of view, at least on the surface. Most of these were British, for understandable reasons; as the ally with the "special relationship" with Washington, and also as the ally that tended to share American preoccupations with keeping the continent under control from a distance, London found much to admire in the American approach. But smaller NATO members, like Norway, Iceland, and Denmark, objected to being pushed so rapidly into militant anti-Soviet postures; France and Italy found themselves unwilling and unable to meet the force levels the United States insisted they maintain, and West Germany remained outside NATO. American policy had created the organization it demanded, but at a rather high price in ill feeling. What's more, the United States blithely continued to believe that Europeans generally accepted the unanswerable wisdom of each element in the American formula.

The Failure of the EDC

In the American view, the major gap in NATO was the absence of Germany. As a battleground for the "forward strategy" and as a potential source of valuable military manpower, Germany was vital to the American scheme of things European.

Washington had been committed to German rearmament ever since 1949 but had encountered at least three sets of objections. The first had come from the Soviet Union, which made it clear from the outset that it would regard German rearmament as a highly provocative act. The second came from European allies that had suffered German occupation during the war and were not eager to forgive and forget. Finally, major resistance to rearmament came from the people of West Germany itself, as the vaunted "military tradition" turned out to be a substantial casualty of the Hitler era.

But no one can accuse the American government of lack of persistence in dealing with such objections; apparently, making a policy decision is so difficult that once the line is laid down in Washington, no effort is spared in following it. German rearmament became an end in itself, at least in the minds of some American planners. After several schemes had aborted, the Pléven Plan for a European Defense Community—a common European army—seemed to provide the ideal solution. Once the project passed the negotiating stage and was submitted for ratification to the parliaments of the six nations involved, American pressure politics swung into action.

Lobbying may or may not be an American invention, but it has certainly been refined to a remarkable degree in the United States. Washington made it unmistakably clear that the EDC should be swiftly ratified by all parties. With all possible delicacy it reminded its associates of the benefits of its generosity and protection when times were hard and the Soviet threat great—implying that deliberate flouting of a benefactor is stupid and dangerous. Partly as a result of American pressure, but probably more because the treaty itself seemed like the best way to reinvigorate Europe's defenses while reintegrating West Germany into the community of European states, the treaty was quickly ratified by five of its signatories. In France, however, the very place of its birth, it came to grief.

The rejection of the EDC treaty by the National Assembly of the Fourth Republic left American policy toward German rearmament temporarily stranded: direct rearmament was politically unacceptable in several quarters, and now the European-army formula had been junked. At this point the United States received a pay-off from its cultivation of Great Britain. The British government, under the leadership of Sir Anthony Eden, took strong initiatives to salvage the situation while the United States—for the first time since 1945, and quite grumpily—remained silent and discreet in the background.

The result came to be known immediately as Western European Union. Building upon the Brussels Treaty of 1948, in which Britain, France, and the Benelux states had agreed to act together for common defense, the British government acted to expand this group by inviting Italy and West Germany to join. The enlarged alliance then wrote into the Final Act of the London Meeting in October 1954 a series of limitations on future German rearmament, limitations selected to quiet fears of renewed German aggressiveness by guaranteeing that German arms would forever remain under external scrutiny and control.

Under these terms of the Western European Union agreements, German rearmament was first undertaken (and, as a matter of fact, continues to this day) and the West German government formally acceded to the North Atlantic Treaty. With unusual speed, the transactions that began in London on October 3 were completed twenty days later when a protocol accepting German accession to the treaty was drafted and submitted to members of NATO.

Ratification of the several documents required several months, and it was not until May 5, 1955 (5/5/55—the famous "four fives" of recent German history) that the Federal Republic of Germany took its place in the ranks of NATO members. A major element—perhaps *the* major element—in the European policy of the United States had been successfully brought off. The verdict of V-E Day was in one sense reversed, for Germany was no longer to be considered a defeated enemy but an important and respected ally.

Yet, however important German rearmament was to the United States, the way in which it had been brought about caused further wounds to the sensitive spirit of Atlantic cooperation. In the first place, there was unmistakable evidence in the failure of the EDC that Europe (in the person of France) could successfully defy American wishes and not really suffer as a result. It does not seem fanciful to argue that French success in frustrating the United States in 1954 contributed directly to the decision Paris reached two years later to defy Washington openly in the Suez crisis.

The ultimate decision about West German rearmament, however, was almost entirely a European one, reached by Europeans in a heavily parochial context. There were rumors at the time of the London talks that the British had told the United States to keep quiet, that any American attempt to influence the course of negotiations would be counter-productive and potentially disastrous. One need not be an Anglophobe to imagine the relish with which this message was passed on by British officials; ten years of close association with American self-confidence and zeal had already begun to rub certain British sensibilities slightly raw. It was about this time that a British wit observed that being allied with the United States was very much like "being locked in a small room with a friendly—but drunken—giant."

Although the United States has tended to look on post-war West Germany as uniquely its own creation in a politico-military sense, Western Europeans are somewhat more capable of recalling the original terms of German reinstatement in Europe. France and the Benelux states remain particularly sensitive to their early and continuing roles in the process, while Britain (where anti-German sentiment continues more strongly than in perhaps any other NATO country) remains exceptionally suspicious of German intentions. The long and intimate friendship between Washington and Bonn, which began almost immediately after West Germany was admitted to NATO and has continued throughout the Adenauer era well into the Erhard government, has been far from a stabilizing factor in intra-alliance relations. It is, in fact, one of the more deeply buried but continually exacerbating elements of European-American tension today. Not all of NATO's members trust German good will as extensively as the United States seems to do.

Finally, the United States thrust to achieve German rearmament was linked with its earlier determination to militarize the entire European theater, at least in European eyes. The formation of NATO and the rapidity of German rearmament were both criticized as one-dimensional simplifications of a complex problem, making serious East-West negotiation (something the British and—to a lesser extent—some of the smaller allies were already urging) much less likely. The French saw the entire operation as essentially futile and continued their standard alliance policy of lip service, minimal commitment, and pronounced unilateralism.

Contemporary criticism of United States policy in Europe as rigid, militaristic, and unsophisticated is by no means a product of the de Gaulle era. It has been a constant element in the transatlantic dialogue and a modifying factor in Europe's reception of American moves since 1951. The EDC was more than America's first real failure in Europe; it marked the beginning of overt resistance and occasional revolt against the pre-eminent role of the United States that has reached full flower in the mid-1960's.

The Suez Crisis and Its Aftermath

The troubles that began for the United States in 1951 finally boiled over in the Suez crisis in 1956. From the point of view of Atlantic relations, and not as a Middle East or a

Cold War issue, that tangled episode was neither an isolated and unexpected incident nor the result of a single mistake by Secretary Dulles. In fact, it was a logical outgrowth of both the course of inter-allied relationships and the evolution of the Soviet-American confrontation. It was an early symptom of divergent Atlantic attitudes, policies, and interests.

By 1956 certain developments in Western Europe had, in the eyes of such key states as Britain and France, made it necessary to recognize a drastically changed situation. In the first place, the military confrontation in Western Europe had eased under the effects of the dawning weapons stalemate and the "spirit of Geneva." Actually, the self-denying ordinance Khrushchev and Bulganin had exchanged with Eisenhower at Geneva in 1955—that neither would be the first to attack with nuclear weapons—was in Anglo-French eyes no more than an affirmation of the obvious. Thus, Britain and France—actually, all the Western European states—felt that they had acquired a new freedom of action to pursue their own interests, simply because the two nuclear giants had openly admitted their unwillingness to go to war with each other.

This brought London and Paris to confront the phenomenon of Nasser in the Middle East under greatly changed conditions. London, Paris, and Jerusalem held no illusions that the United States would sanction a direct military attack on Egypt, but they counted on the nuclear stalemate to confine Washington to verbal protests for fear of provoking Soviet counter-action; while the United States was lamenting the aggression, they reasoned, the canal zone would fall.

This seems most un-ally-like behavior, and indeed it was. But Britain and France were both restive under American leadership in Europe, feeling that Washington was insensitive to their own problems and interests. Both also apparently saw the stalemate of the Cold War in Europe as a testimonial to the success of the alliance and saw nothing contrary to NATO policy in their actions outside the treaty area. Both also knew that Washington's view of the alliance was more than slightly one-sided; the United States hopes for and expects support from its allies in any undertakings it may launch anywhere (such as Vietnam), without feeling a reciprocal obligation toward its associates. NATO, in other words, supports American policies, but not necessarily those of its smaller members.

All of this suggests that Britain and France in 1956 acted on a much more traditional view of alliance than the United States was willing to accept. Both London and Paris found it necessary not only to keep secrets from Washington but actually to deceive the United States about their intentions and preparations with regard to the Suez venture. To the Washington of Dwight Eisenhower and John Foster Dulles, this was perhaps the unkindest cut of all: the two key allies of the United States were prepared to deal with America as an enemy.

Much nonsense has been written about American policy during the Suez imbroglio, both in the United States and elsewhere. Whatever criticisms may be leveled at the Eisenhower-Dulles line, there is not the slightest merit in the argument that the better approach for the United States would have been to follow the British (and, to a lesser extent, the French) lead throughout the Suez affair—up to and including active if covert support of the military invasion. In no discernible way would such a course have been in the interest of the United States, nor would the climate of alliance relations have been especially improved thereby. Meek American submission to Anglo-French initiatives in the Middle East would only have guaranteed future European attempts to cash American blank checks until the point of vanishing returns was finally reached. It was just as well for the vigor of the Atlantic alliance that the challenge was met squarely the first time it arose.

Not so harmless were the tactics the United States used against its allies. Had the U.S. openly concerted with the Soviet Union to present a common great-power opposition to London and Paris, the latter two governments—although resentful—would have understood; this is the way the game of power politics has been played in the past. But the actual American policy—mobilizing an ill-assorted collection of small states under the aegis of the General Assembly of the United Nations, while making *sub rosa* contacts with the Soviets—infuriated the French and at least some dominant elements in the British government almost beyond restraint. Sir Anthony Eden became ill and nearly inarticulate in his rage at what he viewed as American duplicity. It seems clear in retrospect that French decisions that NATO had finally become expendable had their origins in the Suez affair.

It is difficult to believe that the United States has not yet grasped the clear lesson of the Suez crisis, even though it left its mark on an entire generation of Americans. The "disarray" into which the alliance fell in 1956 was seen by Washington as harmful, even though similar disagreement had been overlooked regularly for half a decade. It was quite evident that no one in Washington had any idea of how to avoid disarray in the future—as long as it was accepted as a basic postulate that American policy in Europe was unchangeable and beyond serious discussion.

There were those in 1956 (although not so many as were to appear in later years) who contended that NATO unity was so critical to America's European policy that the United States should make any concession to keep its allies happy. Except with regard to West German–American relations, however, this remained a minority view, popular only among revisionists anxious to pillory John Foster Dulles and his work. As a guide to on-going policy, this idea opens the United States to constant blackmail by its smaller associates. But if giving in to allies is an overexpensive way of preserving unity, what other course is more hopeful?

There are two possible answers. The first is for the United States to adapt its own formulas to an allied consensus and be prepared to proceed only to the extent of agreement that prevails at the moment. This is the approach that the United States has never been able to implement in Atlantic relations. It calls for constancy in purpose and objectives, great flexibility in tactics, a high priority for over-all goals and a low one for particular programs, and vigorous exploitation of agreement coupled with studied avoidance of divisive or stalemating situations. The second approach is in fact the one the United States adopted: patient reiteration of established positions, in the hope that time or the processes of history would restore recalcitrant allies to their senses.

Since Suez the United States has not significantly modified its alliance policy and has continued to exploit the lines laid down before 1956. This has meant, more than anything else, military "strengthening" of NATO; in turn, since the other major European allies have never met their force levels, this has involved the magnification of West Germany's politico-military role in the alliance. So pronounced did pro-German sentiment become in at least parts of the American government that by the mid-1960's some Washington voices were urging that future American policy rest on a German-American "special relationship," with France abandoned as a hopelessly hostile adversary of the alliance and Britain relegated to second-level status because of its weaknesses.

But all to no avail. "Disarray" on the 1956 model has been the norm of the alliance ever since Suez, even though overt policy break-outs like that adventure have been avoided. The United States still presents itself to Europe as the architect of a common position, common policy, and common programs on all questions facing the alliance—especially, of course, that of an approach to the Soviet Union —when in fact such unity has never existed and certainly does not exist today.

If two major U.S. allies were convinced a decade ago of the primacy of their own interests over the myth of alliance solidarity, and if they and other allies have since shown that all absolutist implications of American alliance theory find few takers in Europe, it seems that history is trying to tell the United States something. Suez indicated that the American approach to Europe was lacking in some important respects, and that restoration of anything like the earlier euphoria would require a major overhaul of the U.S. formula.

Thus, the contemporary crisis grows not out of the specific issues of Suez, nor of the temporary animosities generated there. But Suez provided an accurate forecast of the shape of things to come, and the inability of the United States to read the moral so clearly pointed at the time has led to a series of further self-perpetuating misjudgments and missteps. Contemporary policy-makers are struggling today with the consequences.

Differing Approaches to the Soviet Union

Since the Geneva summit conference of 1955 and the Suez crisis of 1956, one of the major rifts in the structure of alliance relationships has been over perception of the Soviet threat and how best to cope with it. Here, as we have seen earlier, the United States has pursued a double role that some Europeans see as one of duplicity.

On another level, however, the quarrel within the alliance about how best to deal with the Soviet Union has only underscored an old truth: the lot of the leader of an alliance—like that of a policeman—is not a happy one. American policy is often attacked by some of its European critics, especially in Britain and Scandinavia, as being overly militant in its approach to Moscow; in Germany, however, a more frequent charge is that the United States is willing to sacrifice German interests to obtain an agreement with the Soviets—an agreement, furthermore, that is doomed to fail. French critics tend to share both these positions: they accuse America of having a phobia about communism on the one hand and profess to see a sinister intent in American attempts to regularize Soviet-American relations on the other. These two lines come together in the Gaullist canard that the United States no longer believes in the reality of the Cold War but attempts to use the rhetoric of fear to perpetuate its hegemony over its European allies.

But, intra-alliance one-upmanship aside, there has clearly been a gradual and steady divergence of views within the alliance since the mid-1950's about how best to cope with the Soviet Union. Generally, also, the United States has been cast in the role of defending the hard line toward Moscow, while in one way or another Europeans have argued for greater flexibility.

There is no particular point of view toward the Soviets that is "European." The several states of Western Europe differ among themselves on this basic point, and no single European country is unified completely within itself on the issue—any more than the United States is. Probably the most useful way to understand the split is first to distinguish various national positions.

Among the larger members of NATO, Great Britain has been most consistent in urging relaxation and major initiatives for negotiation. American doctrine claims, for example, that the Geneva summit conference of 1955 was a complete failure because it solved no concrete problems. But Britons think that since 1955 there has been a major shift in Soviet policy in Europe, and that prospects for significant agreement with Moscow are good enough to warrant a serious approach by the West, with substantial concessions as a basis for bargaining over European issues. British policy has tried for a decade to mollify, soften, and inhibit U.S. anti-Soviet stands (while at the same time attempting to obstruct an overdose of pro-German moves and commitments).

At the opposite extreme from the British—and possibly a contributing factor to continuing Anglo-German tension —is the West German position of ostensibly uncompromising militancy toward the Soviet Union until it accedes to Germany's legitimate demands for reunification and free association with the West. Bonn's rigidity on Soviet policy is a monument to Konrad Adenauer, and especially to his close and profitable working relationship with John Foster Dulles. Whether Adenauer was ever as crusading about his anti-Soviet commitments as was Dulles may never be proved, but he and the American Secretary of State found it rewarding in the mid-1950's to vie in hurling imprecations in the general direction of the Kremlin on the slightest provocation.

Under Erhard, however, the main concern of the German government is no longer the maintenance of close ties with Washington, and Adenauer's valedictory in 1966, when he stepped down from the chairmanship of the Christian Democratic Union, cast grave doubts on the sincerity of Bonn's entire hard-line posture. (These doubts were strengthened in mid-1966 when the parliamentary leader of the CDU made a radical proposal for German reunification that would provide for continued Soviet and allied occupation of the new German state for as long as necessary to prove

German good faith.) Dr. Adenauer apparently discovered that the Soviet Union had "joined the ranks" of the states of the world who are actively seeking peace. Although disclaimers were hastily offered by Bonn officials, the fatal words had been uttered and their consequences were portentous: of what use is militancy against a peace-loving and non-aggressive Soviet Union? If Adenauer's views gain major currency in German society, one of the few remaining underpinnings of American policy will be washed away.

France's attitude toward the Soviet Union has been much more equivocal. Certainly under de Gaulle, heir of much of the right-wing political fervor of the Fourth Republic, there is little ground for accusing France's policy of being "soft on communism" or of minimizing the Soviet threat. On the other hand, the general's faith in the "grand tradition" of statecraft has led him to sneer at America's ideological fixation on communism; he thinks the Soviet Union can be effectively dealt with by diplomatic maneuver and adjustments of national interest. Thus, France is interested in American guarantees against Soviet attack less as an immediate protection than as a shield against a remote contingency.

The smaller members of NATO tend to divide on this issue according to their own interests and histories. Scandinavian members, seeing NATO primarily as an umbrella against possible Soviet attack and wanting it to be no more, line up with Britain in urging moderation and compromise. The Benelux countries emphasize the internal evolution of Western Europe rather than the East-West confrontation. Portugal has been quite vociferously anti-communist but fortunately has not been called upon to translate this into action. Greece and Turkey, at least until the Cyprus question diverted their attention, were quite comfortably installed in the camp of the verbal hard-liners and, especially in the case of Turkey, were prepared to back up their statements. Because of this chronically diffused situation, the United States has usually been able to count on some support for almost any position it cares to adopt. This has bred something of a false sense of security among American policy-makers: no matter what the exigencies of the moment might demand, Washington has trusted in its ability to mobilize a consensus at least to prevent the formation of a clearly hostile majority in the alliance.

By and large, American policy has favored maximum "tautness" in Soviet-American relations—or has interpreted events in the most negative acceptable terms. In so doing, the United States has been opposed by more of its European allies than have supported it. On every one of the relatively few issues of direct East-West confrontation in Europe—of which the status and future of Berlin has perhaps been the most taxing—the United States (generally supported by West Germany) has insisted upon maximizing the crisis and the showdown, while the European allies (led by Britain and the smaller states) have been optimistic about peaceful compromise and the solution of outstanding issues.

The 1960's have seen a major U.S. effort to modify the climate of Soviet-American relations; John Kennedy and Lyndon Johnson have both emphasized damping down of the Cold War in Europe as a prerequisite to survival. But Washington has been unable to reconcile this laudable effort at great-power politics with its long-standing doctrine of alliance, and this inability has aroused confusion and ill feeling in both directions across the Atlantic. By the same token, the rise of Red China to the status of primary enemy of the United States has again posed serious problems of alliance relationships: the U.S. both wants and feels it deserves support from its NATO allies in its anti-Chinese policies, and it is baffled and resentful when Europe's response is weak and equivocal.

The Politico-Military Dilemma of the 1960's

When all is said and done, the crux of the North Atlantic crisis is a question of function. Is the task of the Western coalition primarily a political one, or is it basically military? Should the alliance concentrate on the defense of the West in a largely military sense, or do NATO and its potential appendages have a positive political role to play?

Of course the alliance is political in intent and outlook— as any alliance must be; shared values and goals are the only possible cement of joint action. So far everyone agrees. But moving from this high plane of idealism to the practical levels of planning and acting in the real world has proved impossible for NATO. Its present racked condition is one result.

Again we may spell out—oversimply but not inaccurately —a European-American split. To the United States, all the priority political decisions facing the West in Europe were made between 1946 and 1952, culminating in the decision to contain communism in Europe by force of arms. Alliance policy since that date has been really nothing more than attempts to implement these basic decisions. The Soviet threat, although admittedly diminished, still requires the constant energies of the alliance—indefinitely, or at least until a "victory" is achieved. Thus, military questions growing out of a basic political consensus remain in American eyes the major business of the alliance.

This formula seems simplistic to a number of European NATO members. Charles de Gaulle has been the principal dissenter, but his Fifth Republic is not alone in challenging the institutional and military arrangements so dear to the United States. Indeed, over the years only West Germany has consistently supported the American contention that the political goals of the alliance are irrevocably fixed, and the German position has been devastatingly easy to comprehend. After all, the American-formulated purposes of the alliance—especially the central place given to German re-unification in Western strategy—were also the ends of German foreign policy. The French, to reiterate, have always believed that the essential military deterrence of the Soviet threat was accomplished as soon as the treaty was signed and ratified; given the success of this deterrent mission, French theorists discount the alliance as the basis for a fighting coalition and cast the goals of the organization in purely political terms.

As we have seen already, one of the casualties of American insistence on emphasizing the military role of NATO has been any real consultation among its members on policy decisions. With all important decisions already made in Washington more than a decade ago, the only remaining issues are technical and tactical. So there is little reason for the United States to consult broadly with its allies. American pre-eminence seems clear to Washington, and the United States has felt fully justified in unilaterally shifting NATO's military policy to allow for domestic considerations (such as the introduction of "flexible response" in 1962) or to meet the demands of policy in other parts of the world (such as Vietnam).

Europeans clearly resent being left out of the consultative process. France attempted to capture some of its lost status in 1958 by proposing a NATO "directorate," to be composed of Britain, France, and the United States, that would develop a common policy and posture for the alliance, not only in Europe but in the whole non-Western world as well. The United States rejected the proposal in what can only be characterized as a brusque manner, yet for simple reasons: Washington was not prepared to admit Paris as an equal in policy-making, was not willing to allow West

Germany to be so clearly frozen out, and was not even close to agreement with basic French contentions that any new apparatus for policy-making was desirable.

Failure of the French suggestion even to receive serious consideration in Washington (or in London, for that matter) seems finally to have convinced the Quai d'Orsay that further cooperation within the NATO framework would not prove profitable. The secessionist line that President de Gaulle has pursued ever since had its origin in the sour aftermath of what the French apparently saw as a serious and well-meaning initiative. And it is strange that eight years after its rejection of the French proposal, Washington, desperately trying to find a means of coping with a recalcitrant France and of adding European support to its Asian policy at the same time, proposed that West Germany, Britain, and the United States form a common policy-making body for NATO—in other words, a "directorate."

The history of the past two decades in Atlantic relations illustrates the constant primacy of politics. Politics, defined practically as the collective pursuit of value satisfaction in a context of disagreement, is not a technical subject as are military issues; it is an art, not a science. The persistent attempt of the United States to "quantify" its problems with Western Europe, so that military and economic issues can be dealt with in a "scientific manner," has brought only frustration and disappointment to Washington. The dominant concern of the North Atlantic community is no longer a military one; politics has again taken over.

Chapter Six
The Crisis: The European-American Rift

Trouble and disarray have been NATO's lot almost from the moment of its birth, but the contemporary rift in the Atlantic world is the most critical in its history. American policy-makers and American public opinion now finally admit that all is not well in NATO. Skilled almost beyond any other people in hearing only what they want to hear, Americans for a long time were able to overlook or ignore clear signs of tension. Those few observers—academics, journalists, or statesmen—who during the 1950's suggested a fresh look at the reality of Europe, were crushed under the weight of hostile rejoinders flowing from the Establishment and its defenders.

Yet by 1966 it was no longer fashionable to blame all the problems of the alliance on the shortsightedness, the megalomania, or the jealousy of Charles de Gaulle; a somewhat broader perspective had begun to seep into government circles and other informed quarters. The thorough review that American policy needs may yet become possible. State Department officials were admitting in 1966, in speeches and press briefings, that perhaps some American policies in Europe had grown a bit "long in the tooth," or that perhaps the "conduct of Atlantic affairs has gotten into a rut." These were signs that a few shafts of light were beginning to penetrate what had been for years a closed and dark chamber of policy.

But we must be as realistic as possible. Coupled with these occasional admissions that some fault may lie with U.S. policy and past behavior (admissions that are the more remarkable because they flow from quarters that never in the memory of living man have admitted shortcomings in American policy, most noticeably the Bureau of Public Affairs of the Department of State), there remains a staunch defense of the basic ingredients of the American approach. Thus, a peculiar ambivalence affects and dilutes the impact of contemporary American versions of *"mea culpa";* by confining confession of error to peripheral issues or administrative minutia, the essentials of the existing policy and its administrative ethos can be preserved for a while longer.

The best one can manage as of this writing is a guarded optimism about a breakthrough in American policy. The verdict is still out, and official American recipes tend with weary consistency to be minor variations on the theme of "come home, come home, ye who have (temporarily) strayed." As far as the major offender is concerned, France has refused to accept a place under the wing of American power as "home" in any useful sense.

The Nature of the Crisis

Generally, the American position today assumes that European-American problems take place within an institutional framework and are more than anything else matters of organization. So there are problems in NATO, problems in the OECD, problems in and with the EEC, and so on. Implicitly, policy *premises* are left unchallenged, differences are assumed to be procedural, and arguments used by Washington take on an illusory concreteness. The organizational approach also allows American officials to easily score debater's points at the expense of other states; France's objections to NATO are frequently dismissed as "abstract," "ambiguous," or "theoretical." And dissenters who cannot gain a hearing for "theoretical" arguments with the status quo are told to make their proposals "concrete." By rejecting organizational changes, the United States fulfills its purpose of defending the status quo.

It seems astonishing, for example, that serious and intelligent American policy-makers should have allowed themselves to be so grossly misled by the non-issue of "nuclear sharing" in NATO. All American proposals in this area really intend to preserve an effective U.S. monopoly over the decision to use nuclear weapons. The entire effort has been aimed from the beginning directly at the French view of the alliance and, incidentally, has had the secondary goal of winning more votes in the popularity contest in West Germany, in which the State Department has long felt itself engaged with the Quai d'Orsay.

Another example of the institutional fallacy in American crisis policy was the U.S. response to France's announcement in early 1966 that it intended to withdraw from all integrated military commands of NATO, and that it expected all NATO headquarters on French soil to be vacated forthwith. American rejoinders during the first few weeks were discouragingly predictable: France was warned that the United States might "revise and reduce" its commitment to France's defense, and might specifically deny the French use of NATO's early-warning air defense system. No threat calculated further to inflame French sensibilities, or less likely to have an effect on French policy, could have been selected. General de Gaulle was acting out of a conviction that the likelihood of America's having to defend France had been sharply reduced. Furthermore, both Gallic logic and a glance at the map argued that it was nonsensical for the United States to threaten to allow France to fall to communism while continuing to defend the rest of the NATO area. Yet this is precisely what the United States did threaten.

If, contrary to the American approach, the Atlantic crisis is not one of institutional or organizational forms, what in fact is its essential nature? The United States has had little success in improving matters by tinkering with structures. How deeply must it go before it can hope to strike pay dirt?

The answer seems to be "very deeply." As Europeans see it, the crisis is one of an evolving status relationship between the two parts of the alliance, a readjustment of intra-alliance dynamics to reflect more accurately the positions all members occupy today.

In specific terms, Europeans—led by France—are seeking repeal of those cherished American symbols of "Atlantic cooperation," most explicitly the integration of command in NATO. To repeat: France has made the most extreme statements and taken the most extreme positions in this effort, but every member of NATO in Europe—including, as we have seen, West Germany—is aware of the need for rethinking and restructuring the working relationship between a newly proud and self-confident Europe and its

American protector. But Washington is simply not willing to admit this basic need.

This is a political judgment, although of course it has a military fallout. The new equality Europeans seek is expressible only in political, cultural, and economic terms. It carries no implication that Europe—even a possible united Europe, something no one foresees in the near future—will be able independently to "defend" itself against the Soviet Union. American arguments make much of this point, but Europeans normally concede it as self-evident and dismiss it as irrelevant.

Such a sanguine approach to Europe's military inferiority rests on two assumptions, neither of which the United States has discovered how to challenge. The first is the waning of European fear of Soviet attack, a basic modification in the operational (as opposed to the conceptual) environment that generates major changes in other policy areas. The other root is Europe's—and especially de Gaulle's—belief that the inexorable forces of history and national interest commit the United States to defend Europe against Soviet attack forever, regardless of the immediate state of European-American relations.

So, in the minds of most European leaders today, the time is ripe to strike for a radical revision of their status vis-à-vis the United States. They see themselves engaged in only the first step of what will necessarily be a fairly extensive process of readjustment. Yet they have a twofold problem: they must carry their relations with each other to new levels of coordination and integration, while at the same time they must develop a common and effective approach to the United States. They must do this, furthermore, during an historic era when the possibility of nuclear holocaust cannot be entirely dismissed, however much it may be downgraded. Such a task requires basic changes rivaling the "diplomatic revolutions" of earlier centuries, yet Europeans do not seek a revolution.

Instead of a massive change of partners within the alliance, Europe would probably insist that it is aiming for a revolution in the general compass of the Atlantic community, a shift in status and role for NATO members. It is not clear, furthermore, that Western Europe's aspirations are in fact inimical to American interests, as is so often suggested in Washington. This book argues the contrary: not only is a new European-American relationship inevitable, given contemporary trends in Europe and the world, but it will also prove to be more profitable for the United States as well. Superior diplomatists have always been characterized by their ability to get the practical maximum of *what they wanted* from any particular context. There is a lesson in this principle for the United States; contemporary policymakers seem to be groping toward it in many parts of the world.

Washington must always remember that France's leading role in the European revolt has not been without support. No member of the Atlantic alliance is satisfied with the place it occupies vis-à-vis the United States, and each is angling subtly and deftly to improve its position. For every declaration of support against France that Washington has been able to wring from the other thirteen members of NATO, the United States has been obliged to pay in the coin of status—frequently, as a matter of fact, with precisely the symbols America has long denied France.

But by 1966 the crisis had acquired another dimension, too. It is clear, for instance, that de Gaulle's policy is partly to repudiate and humiliate the United States. It would appear that this is seen as a desirable end in itself, even though the French know that too strong a hand may produce undesirable—and equally irrational—American responses.

This proved to be the case when France finally took the long-predicted step and vowed its determination "to get France out of NATO and NATO out of France." American replies were sharp, French ripostes equally acerbic, and within a few weeks the climate of discussion—especially in the less responsible press of both countries—had left judiciousness and reason behind.

The Military Dilemma

The European crisis bothers Americans most as a challenge to free-world arrangements for the military defense of Western Europe. In American eyes, all issues of European-American relations finally come down to the preservation of NATO essentially intact and the price America must pay.

But an alliance does not exist *in vacuo;* it must be an instrument of common response to a threat that is perceived in basically the same way by all its members. At this primary point the American attempt to "save"—let alone strengthen—NATO comes to grief. The United States must contend, if its theory of alliance is to have any validity at all, that the Soviet threat has not abated since 1949 in any important respect. No European statesman today accepts this American argument at face value, and as a result the U.S. position is weakened by a predilection for exaggeration.

One recent formulation of the American position is worth quoting at length here. It comes from a highly qualified source outside the executive branch: the Senate Subcommittee on National Security and International Operations, known widely as the "Jackson Committee" after its chairman, Senator Henry Jackson of Washington. Its report on the problems of the alliance, issued in April 1966, was marked by some of the new realism that we noted earlier; the staff members who prepared the study made a valiant effort to note at least some of the minor failings of American policy.

But not too many. In every important way, *The Atlantic Alliance: Basic Issues* (the report's official title) accepts as beyond question prevailing American doctrine and calls upon Europe—especially France—to mend its erring ways. On the matter that concerns us here, the divergent interpretation of the Soviet threat, the report saves its simplest and most sweeping formulation for its conclusion:

> Now, as in 1949, the foundation of the Alliance is a working agreement among the allies on what the Soviet threat is and how to deal with it—together. (p. 6)

This conclusion is reached by logic that is fascinating in its simplicity. Only a lengthy quotation can do justice to the argument:

> The failure to obtain a [European] settlement is not to be explained by a refusal of the West to recognize the legitimate interests of the Soviet Union. It is not to be explained by a lack of imagination in the West. It is not, as some now find it fashionable to say, a lack of "bright ideas" or "brilliant policy proposals" but a lack of Soviet interest in any terms that do not take as a premise the continued Soviet hold on the Warsaw Pact countries, and, in particular, East Germany. (p. 5)

Thus the American line, hackneyed by overuse in every part of the world: everything would be fine if only the communists were not so evil. There is no need for any new Western policies; the old ones are adequate. Hold fast, comrades, and keep your powder dry!

But some fault can be found with U.S. policy, at least in recent years:

There are some doubts in Western Europe about the steadiness and coherence of American policy toward East-West relations. The United States has not yet brought its foreign receipts and payments into balance, with the result that doubts grow about the financial ability of the United States to support its European policies. In its enthusiasm for a European settlement, the United States government has pursued the will-of-the-wisp of rapprochement with the Soviet Union, even though this raises in Western Europe, especially in West Germany, the specter of bilateral Soviet-American deals at the expense of European interests. . . . An obvious danger is that major concessions will be made on our side without any compensating change of policy on the Soviet side. (pp. 5–6)

This paragraph, wrapping up much American dogma in a few lines, bears rereading a few times. There are "doubts" in Western Europe about the "steadiness and coherence" of the American approach to the Soviet Union; rapprochement is a "will-of-the-wisp" that West Germany fears; the only possible deals are at Germany's expense (for "European interests" in this particular argument we must of course read "West German interests," particularly in the Oder-Neisse line and the lost provinces in the East). Finally, the argument rests on the irrefutable basis that, because Soviet diplomats are much more clever than their American counterparts, a major swindle is always a danger. The only way to guard against it is for the United States never to negotiate alone—truly an impressive defense of the need for alliance unity!

But the argument is not yet complete:

For the United States to show unsureness and unsteadiness in its perception of the continuing Soviet threat is especially disturbing. Despite the remarkable recovery of the Western European allies, they do not have, separately or jointly, the strength to counter Soviet pressures. For the United States to toy with the idea of rapprochement, therefore, is to tempt its allies into unilateral exploration of the possibilities of transforming *their* relations with the Soviet Union—and thus to create new opportunities for Soviet diplomacy to achieve what Soviet arms and pressures have been unable to win. (p. 7)

So now we have it: the United States is at bottom to blame for de Gaulle's initiatives toward Moscow, and would be to blame if Bonn were to go to Moscow itself. So essential is it for America to keep its allies away from the Kremlin, the argument goes, that even Washington itself should not "toy" (a very well-chosen pejorative term, coupling frivolity with risk) with any negotiations. The conclusion seems difficult to avoid that a real peace settlement in Europe would be almost as much of a disaster for American policy as a major war, for true peace would signal the breakup of the alliance once and for all. Every other undertaking in Europe, the report contends, including all attempts at arms control and an anti-proliferation treaty, should be junked for fear that one of them might prove unexpectedly successful, thus undercutting the basic American reason for being in Europe at all.

Most any comment on this line of argument would be superfluous; its own logic is self-sustaining and its eloquence compelling. In essence, it commits the United States to defend NATO as it was in 1949, as the major element in its European—and perhaps its global—policy. Alliance unity at all costs is the watchword, and maintenance of good will with Germany—"keeping Bonn happy with its bargain"— is the theme. Two threads run through the entire report: one, predictably, is an anti-French bias; the other, as we have already suggested, is a strong pro-German proclivity. Later in the report, a brief discussion of the "nuclear questions [that] are troubling and dividing the allies" is included. The report admits that the problems are "complex" but insists that "the time is past, certainly, for trying to deal with this problem on the basis that our European allies are equal but that one is less equal than the others" (p. 11). So much, therefore, for the Treaty of Western European Union and the terms on which Germany entered NATO!

Again, threat perception is a political and not a military exercise. In matters of national strategy involving the use of nuclear weapons, the issues of survival, and the commitment of major increments of national resources, no state— not even the United States—can expect to deal with *all possible* contingencies. It must make its analyses in terms of *relative probabilities* and its own priority of purposes. Thus, when Europeans hear official American arguments such as the one we have quoted here, they assume that the United States has a political (i.e., value-oriented) purpose in mind; they simply cannot believe that the most powerful nation in the world can *really* be persuaded that no change has occurred in Soviet intentions toward Europe, and that only a 1949-type response can be risked in the 1960's. Something else, they say, must be at work in American planning, and here de Gaulle's vocabulary of "vassalage," "subordination," and so on comes easily to mind.

But we must not overestimate the sophistication of American policy-makers, even though Europeans may do so. American foreign policy is filled with too many examples of blind faith in twenty-year-old decisions and impressive organizations for us to assume that a clear-eyed Machiavellianism is at work. Simple bureaucratic inertia is much more likely. It is easier to argue that "nothing fundamental has changed" in the European situation, and that therefore no modifications of the NATO posture are necessary, than to begin a painful reevaluation and restructuring of a new policy line. Even defenders of American policy can be induced to confess specific operational failures, which suggests that little more than habit underlies existing American policy in Europe.

The military dilemma of the alliance can be simply stated: nothing fails like success. Regardless of NATO's role as a corporate entity in the changing political climate in Europe, the military task originally set for the alliance in 1949 has certainly been accomplished. The armed threat to Western Europe from Moscow has shrunk to its irreducible minimum. What is there left for NATO to do?

American orthodoxy answers that the United States must maintain the unity and readiness of the alliance in the face of all temptations, until finally the Soviet Union has realized the futility of its effort at hegemony. There is nothing, in either a military or a political way, that the Western alliance can do to speed the process, since a European settlement is contingent upon Moscow's abandonment of most of its postwar policy in Europe. NATO, therefore, must be strong, firm, and patient while waiting for Moscow to change its basic ways.

But this formula of strength, firmness, and patience gives the alliance nothing at all to do. This American preference for passivity, for manipulating empty institutional forms rather than actively searching for some new set of common goals and strategies, has disillusioned many Europeans. Why, they ask, go to the expense and trouble to respond to a declining threat?

The Jackson Committee dealt with this problem in language almost dark with foreboding:

> . . . there is as yet no hard evidence that the Soviet Union has given up the contest for Western Europe, or abandoned its goal to break up the association of

Western Europe and North America, or is ready to turn to serious efforts to settle the basic political conflicts with the West. On the contrary, the contest for Europe—in low key for the moment—is still with us, and Soviet forces remain in the center of Europe. The Soviet government continues to invest an increasing share of its resources in arms, to push for major advances in critical new weapons, and to reject internationally inspected and controlled arrangements for the limitation of arms. (p. 4)

The committee, after warning that "we cannot be confident" that a Soviet Union marked by internal freedom would be less interested in world conquest, "nor can we discount the danger" that polycentrism in Eastern Europe "will lead to new forms of crisis to which the West has given little thought" (the report points out that "there is always the possibility" that Moscow might attempt to restore unity to Eastern Europe by manufacturing a German crisis), then turns to Sino-Soviet relations:

Nor does the discord between Moscow and Peking necessarily increase the likelihood of substantive settlements in Europe. In fact, the incessant Chinese criticism of Soviet leadership as insufficiently militant, and whatever gains for Red China her combativeness may produce, are generating pressures on Moscow to demonstrate its own militancy. . . . Soviet leaders, of course, are not unconcerned with Chinese expansionism. . . . But we cannot assume that Moscow and Peking are headed for a final separation. In time, with the passing from the scene of Mao Tse-tung, some reconciliation is conceivable. (p. 4)

These selections provide a representative sampling of American "action rhetoric." Unable and unwilling to deny the reality of change, Americans talk about vague, slippery, and portentous "possibilisms." All figure prominently in the American effort to argue that—at least for the purposes of the alliance—the immediate military danger posed by the Soviets is unchanged.

But European members of NATO no longer accept the American thesis that NATO is primarily a military instrument, and they simply cannot accept the logic of possibilism. They seek a broader role for the alliance than one merely of watchful waiting.

Thus, the United States has found itself unable to break the deadlock besetting NATO today. The best Washington has been able to do in recent years is to try to confront some of the more "practical" military problems of the alliance. One dear to the hearts of the Kennedy and Johnson administrations has been the risk of nuclear proliferation, spelled out in alliance terms as a series of attempts to deny France the opportunity to develop its own limited nuclear capability. The major vehicle for this effort has been the multilateral (inter-allied) nuclear force—known to the press as MLF.

MLF was the darling of a small group in the State Department which pursued the project from the beginning of 1961 to the end of 1964 with an almost evangelical zeal. It was a simple and—the United States insisted—workable concept: a fleet of surface vessels (originally submarines in the first proposal, but the problems were greater, and the shift was made) carrying Polaris missiles. These ships would have multi-national crews and be under NATO "jurisdiction," but the final decision to launch the missiles was to be, always, solely American.

The rationale of MLF was to give the German people a "sense of participation" in nuclear matters while simultaneously denying them any command over atomic weapons or the right to develop their own. Advocates claimed that a secondary mission was to isolate France as the renegade that insisted on a national nuclear force while everyone else went happily along with the United States. Some skeptics pointed out that it would not take very long for the Germans to become dissatisfied with a "sense of participation" that amounted to an admonition of "look, but don't touch." Cynics agreed that this was the case and that the eventual result (and primary purpose) of MLF was to create a situation in which West Germany would demand—and be given —its own atomic weapons.

MLF never won any enthusiastic support in Europe except in Bonn. The French rejected the idea, and the British (not, as we have seen, quite as sanguine about German intentions as the United States) cast about for some other gimmick that might serve the notion of "nuclear sharing" while concealing the grim reality of America's dominant and controlling role. London's contribution was the notion of an allied nuclear force (ANF) of a somewhat more catholic makeup, incorporating no formal national veto.

MLF and ANF shared the same fate: almost total disregard by all Europeans except in the one nation that would have been directly strengthened—the Federal Republic of Germany. During 1964, however, the Johnson administration became more and more militant on the subject of MLF, until Britain's Prime Minister Harold Wilson visited Washington and quietly informed President Johnson that the drive for MLF was in fact counter-productive and— even worse—was tarnishing the administration's image in Europe. With no further ado the whole project was then scuttled, and, despite occasional brave words from the State Department, it remains dead.

Again, the United States did its best to ignore the European desire for equality, to perpetuate its own superior position, to obstruct a reconsideration of military issues because of political realities.

There are other points of military disagreement as well. In Chapter Three we sketched the 1962 change in American strategy from "massive retaliation" to "flexible response." This, we noted, was a decision made purely in response to domestic considerations. The Jackson Committee comments:

> . . . in 1962 the United States abruptly shifted to a strategy of flexible response. There was little or no consultation with our allies, and the shift was explained in terms which, to say the least, caused doubt and confusion about what kind of counterblows the United States might be planning in the event of a Soviet attack on Europe. To some in Europe it looked as though the United States would rather switch than fight. . . . The difficulties thereby created have not yet been overcome, especially perhaps in relations with France, whose President, like most chiefs of state, does not accept short shrift easily. (p. 11)

M. Boscher, the French Rapporteur of the Political Committee of the NATO Parliamentarians Conference in October 1965, reports:

> If the theory of escalated counterattack is based on the assumption that the enemy will be allowed to advance into the heart of Western Germany before total nuclear engagement takes place, as some American military experts have envisaged, it is obviously unacceptable to Europe. . . . It must be emphasized that the absence of any coherent policy on the part of the Alliance in this field is an additional justification, if such were needed, for the existence of national nuclear deterrent forces.

Europeans today widely profess to doubt American determination to defend them; the most popular American reply is to point to U.S. troops in Europe and say, "Wait and see." But doubt—whether sincere or not—remains, and Europeans fear that another unilateral American decision might make them further vulnerable to Soviet attack while making the Pentagon more efficient.

Another military problem was precipitated by France's decision to remove all her forces from NATO's integrated commands and ask the other members of the alliance to remove the "infrastructure" from French soil. The worsening crisis, heightened by heated American responses to French action, called up again all the old arguments about "integration" in the alliance—its merits, demerits, and future worth.

The United States attacked France for following a reactionary course, blindly nationalist and dangerously unilateralist. French opposition to integrated commands was interpreted as an assault on the very principle of coordinated defense.

Through 1966, French replies to American criticisms of their policy did not receive any real hearing in the United States. In vain the French pointed out that they had no intention of denouncing the North Atlantic Treaty and expressed the hope that the NATO Council would retain its seat in Paris. Equally futile was French insistence that even a "conventional alliance" presupposes a fairly advanced and well-established degree of coordination in peacetime, especially insofar as planning and strategic goals are concerned. France did not object to coordination or to joint planning and wished to retain those elements; its purpose in withdrawing from the integrated military command structure was to influence NATO toward a more political basis for relations.

But American policy had drifted into the hands of a group in the State Department known informally as the "theologians": Atlanticists, most of them relatively elderly, whose memories and reputations were indissolubly linked to the great days of NATO, in their minds placed somewhere around 1955. They set about establishing a collision course with France on the issue of integration, quite obviously looking forward to a showdown in which all the other allies would be forced to choose between Paris and Washington. If carefully "orchestrated," such a showdown could have only one outcome: total isolation of France, reconsolidation of the alliance under stronger American leadership, final victory of American concepts, and hopefully the repudiation of President de Gaulle by his own people.

Application of this hard line within the alliance, however, produced meager results. Although the American press immediately began to divide the allies into "hawks" and "doves" on the French issue, the prevailing tone within the alliance was clearly against pushing France to the breaking point. Messages urging restraint and caution began to flow from the capitals of the European allies, subtly making the point that an excess of zeal in Washington could produce cleavages in the solid front the United States was seeking to create against Paris.

But the stubborn question remained: could the United States, particularly in view of extensive emotional and political commitments to the status quo, possibly make the adjustments that alone could restore the alliance to minimum workability, let alone harmony? Would such a reformation of American policy be possible without near catastrophe; would, in other words, the United States be able to develop a politically reliable view of the Atlantic alliance without being humiliated or frightened? As of mid-1966 no one could answer those questions or the many like them that crowded the minds of all concerned.

The Approach to the East

To a large if undefinable extent, the 1966 crisis within the Atlantic alliance involved in a new form the old questions of the boundaries of "Europe" and the approach of Westerners to those behind the Iron Curtain.

By mid-1966 it was clear that Soviet relaxation of tight control over its satellites in Eastern Europe had passed the point of no return. Only East Germany remained under close Soviet supervision, while Poland, Czechoslovakia, Hungary, Rumania, and even Bulgaria moved toward normal relations with Western Europe. There was relatively little evidence of disillusionment with communist systems in Eastern Europe, in spite of the periodic fulminations of the Assembly of Captive European Nations and the regular pounding of Radio Free Europe. The thrust of Eastern Europe to the West was apolitical. Although in large measure economic, perhaps its major component was psychic and cultural. The two halves of Europe, rent asunder by the Cold War, were seeking to rejoin themselves.

This is the prevailing view in the East, and there is no reason to believe that the *Drang nach Westen* of the "socialist bloc" is motivated by opposition to the Soviet Union. On the contrary, although understandably more cautious and less willing to jettison ideological consistency than its minor partners, the Soviet Union has shown in many small ways since 1963 that it too is interested in some forms of non-political identification with the whole of Europe.

Here is where Charles de Gaulle emerges as a European. It is clear that in his Delphic moods, when he is tempted to "dip into the future," he contemplates the much-cited and much-maligned Europe "from the Atlantic to the Urals." As we emphasized before, this is by no means a policy goal for next week, next year, or even for this century; for statesmen in the grand tradition, with whom de Gaulle identifies himself, there is nothing untoward about forecasting for a century hence. Many, many intermediate steps must be taken before this noble concept can boast any hope of realization —and to practical de Gaulle, the unity of Western Europe comes first, even before any tentative moves to the East.

But it is undeniable that the general's espousal of the dream of a reunited Europe—at least in the sense of healing the gaping wounds of the Second World War—has touched a sensitive nerve in the body politic of Western Europe in the 1960's. The split in Europe may be an affront to some Europeans and only an annoyance or minor embarrassment to others; but only the bureaucrats of the ineffable Pankow regime in East Germany have any intrinsic interest in its perpetuation.

There is no doubt that Washington is enthusiastically in favor of broad Soviet-American ties. But does the United States look with favor upon analogous efforts by its smaller European allies?

Ample evidence indicates that the U.S. still maintains its classical position that communism (at least in Europe) is conceptually unified, if no longer truly monolithic. This means that for a smaller European state, such as France, to begin conversations with Rumania about cultural or economic relations is not fundamentally different from Franco-Soviet negotiations on German reunification—and, furthermore, the first type of enterprise may lead with breathtaking suddenness to the second.

The United States cannot in good faith accept the fruits of European détente while denying them to its allies. But every apologist for American policy—if he is frank with himself—must admit that any rapprochement of the two halves of a divided Europe contains the germ of conceptual disaster for the United States. It would be natural for

Washington, while simultaneously protesting its own un-
bounded good will, to try to slow down such a reconciliation, if only as a means of buying valuable time to consider
the future and to devise ways of meeting it.

This problem relates rather directly to the future of
NATO. If the Soviet threat in Europe has indeed been
liquidated, should the alliance simply stand guard duty?
Increasingly, Europeans insist that NATO—or at least the
"alliance"—should take the lead in healing the breach between East and West in Europe.

These proposals have a number of advantages. First,
were the alliance to go East *en bloc* to seek a settlement—
probably through direct dealings with its opposite number,
the Warsaw Pact states—the danger of being swindled
would be correspondingly reduced. Such a move might also
preserve the structural integrity of the alliance during a difficult period, and thereby make its survival and eventual
employment as an instrument of European unity much more
likely.

But these ideas run straight against American dogma, so
they remain anathema in Washington. NATO must remain
based on East-West hostility; to convert it into a mechanism
of reconciliation would prostitute its entire purpose. As a
result, most West European hopes for rapprochement with
East Europe are pinned on the enigmatic figure of Charles
de Gaulle.

Tensions in Trade

Americans generally are prone—perhaps too readily—to
seek the "cash nexus" in every instance of human malad-
justment; to look for economic causes and to prescribe economic cures for most problems of national policy. Atlantic
relations have not been spared this relentless economic

analysis, and undeniably certain economic factors have been at work in the European-American rift.

American policy-makers, as we have seen, were rather slow to accept Europe's economic recovery as a reality. Throughout the 1950's the United States insisted that European economic recovery and continued prosperity depended upon American aid and trade. Late in the decade, however, the growth of the European economy made Europe a highly desirable market for American goods, and American corporations launched a major penetration of the continent.

The success of the EEC and its clearly protectionist overtones alerted the Kennedy administration to the need for a new economic policy toward Europe. This took the form of the New Frontier's widely advertised "Grand Design" for European-American relations, featuring the creation of an "Atlantic Community" (under, of course, American leadership) for trade purposes. This euphemism in practice meant a two-phase reorientation of trade patterns across the North Atlantic and within Europe. Initially, the division of Europe into the EEC (the "Six") and EFTA (the "Seven") was to be healed by British entry into the EEC and the subsequent absorption of the rest of Western Europe into the enlarged Common Market. Then, working through the negotiating mechanisms of GATT, a major round of European-American tariff reduction and liberalization would open the entire North Atlantic community to the benefits of free trade.

As its part of the bargain, the United States would modify its own restrictive tariff legislation. To this end, and in a major administration victory, the Trade Expansion Act of 1962 was passed by a sizable margin in Congress. This freed the President to make linear tariff reductions up to 50 per cent, instead of following the old product-by-product method, and to eliminate all tariffs on products in which at least 80 per cent of the trade goes on between the United States and the EEC.

The Trade Expansion Act was written and passed in expectation that the economic split in Europe would soon be over, with Britain in the Common Market. With Britain in the EEC, a long list of very important products would have been subject to the elimination of all tariffs; with Britain excluded, however, the list dwindled to two products, margarine and jet aircraft. Thus, when President de Gaulle vetoed British entry into the Common Market in January 1963, the rationale of the Grand Design was effectively crippled and the Trade Expansion Act became a monument to a lost cause.

Even before the French decision that Britain was not "European enough" to fit smoothly into the EEC, however, the Grand Design had run into considerable difficulty in Europe. Europeans were quick to notice that the boldest evocations of the new Atlantic Community always included the parenthetical concept—often stated but frequently merely assumed—that this community would remain safely and indefinitely under "American leadership." (The idea of a community had held no attraction for American officials until the growing strength of Europe—particularly the EEC —forced the problem to a higher level of priority.)

Implicit in the New Frontier's thought was a naive hangover from an earlier era of European-American relations, startling in an administration so self-consciously committed to blazing new trails. The Grand Design rested on a simple postulate: Europe needed the United States so much, and U.S. policy was so reasonable and just, that European rejection of the project was unthinkable. The unthinkable was precisely what happened.

In the end, however, de Gaulle's veto of the British application was based on political rather than economic grounds. Coming as it did on the heels of the Nassau agreement that seemed to make Britain a permanent nuclear subordinate of the United States, the press conference made it clear that

Britain's failure to qualify was due not only to its lack of "Europeness" but also to the fact that it was too close to America for any European's comfort. Britain would be the Trojan horse for Americans within Europe, obstructing evolution toward unity and equality vis-à-vis the United States—and de Gaulle would have none of it.

After the French action, the United States remained committed to what had already been labeled the "Kennedy Round" of tariff negotiations within the framework of GATT. American planners had visualized this operation as a triumphant process of creating the Atlantic trading community in a spirit of good will and mutuality of concessions between the United States and the enlarged EEC. Instead, the United States found itself involved in an old-style wrangle about highly complex tariff questions—with only uncertain results waiting at the end of a process almost completely out from under American control.

Two questions remain unanswered for the United States and the Common Market: Will Britain's Labour government bring itself to make serious reapplication in the face of earlier Tory failure and Labour's long-standing anti-European bias? And will France this time accept British membership and the major changes in the EEC that would follow? No satisfactory answers are yet in sight.

Chapter Seven
A New Concept: Political Partnership

By the summer of 1966 even the most calcified bureaucrat in the U.S. Department of State had admitted (at least privately) that the time for major policy reassessments of Atlantic relations had arrived. The old formulas still sounded persuasive in Foggy Bottom; the nation's editorial writers dueled with straw men in their columns; the Establishment vented its spleen on Charles de Gaulle. Yet all the rhetoric was disturbingly reminiscent of King Canute: the United States continued to command the tide to roll back, but it continued to rise. American policy toward Western Europe had, after twenty years, lost its capacity effectively to control events in the Old World, while at the same time it lacked the ability meaningfully to respond to them.

The virtual bankruptcy of American policy in Europe is

due neither to failures of will nor deficiencies of implementation. The trouble lies deeper: the conceptual basis of American policy, laid down in the early post-war era, is now hopelessly out of date; the Europe which the United States tries to pressure today is no longer the Europe of 1946, and policies that worked in 1946 will work no longer. Critics have recognized this for at least half a dozen years, but somehow the practical imperative—that new concepts more appropriate to existing conditions must be established —has escaped the attention of responsible American officials.

This chapter sketches the essentials and touches on a few implications of such a new conceptual base for American foreign policy toward Europe. We call it "political partnership," a term long popular in Western Europe as an antonym to "American leadership," and one that has received increasing attention in the United States in recent months. Whatever specific content future policy-makers may choose to give it, "partnership" seems a sufficiently broad and inclusive notion to cover the ranges of possible European-American coordination and cooperation. Yet it is also specific enough to indicate a pattern of political, military, and economic relations across the Atlantic.

Acceptance of partnership as a basis for American policy requires first that the United States make a difficult and embarrassing admission: the era of American leadership in Europe is over. Europe generally and the major states individually no longer follow voluntarily wherever Washington chooses to go, and the United States lacks both the will and the capability to coerce obedience from reluctant allies.

Militarily the European allies are in revolt against American defense doctrine; politically the allies are demanding new directions and a recalculation of the Soviet threat; economically the new Europe sees itself as competitive rather than complementary to the United States. On no account can the United States any longer assume that its wishes or policies are accepted automatically by its fellows in the West. Instead, Washington must argue for and painfully negotiate partial acceptance of positions it was formerly able to establish unilaterally and virtually without serious discussion.

By 1966 the rationale of American leadership in Europe, which we have already analyzed, had worn extremely thin. West Germany, previously counted on for automatic support of any American position, was no longer as solidly in the American camp as before, seemingly uncertain that Washington would still some day be able to pull the rabbit of unification out of the hat of the Cold War. Latter-day German policy—after the departure of Adenauer—had begun tentatively and hesitatingly to explore hitherto forbidden areas of initiative and concept. What was beginning to be true of the most complaisant European allies had long been self-evident with regard to most others. But few had taken the risky step of openly defying Washington, and the United States drew considerable comfort from the fact that no one else in NATO moved overtly to emulate de Gaulle. All the allies, however, found ways to say that the old formula of American leadership was no longer acceptable and that they intended to pursue their own national interests (and perhaps ultimately Europe's collective interests as well) without feeling any need to defer regularly to American policy.

The American Alternatives

American official rhetoric, especially when used to defend a policy under attack, is fond of the argument that "we had no alternative." However effective this may be in winning arguments between insiders and outsiders (no one outside the Establishment can be completely certain that in a given situation the United States did indeed have an acceptable alternative), in broader terms it is a simple untruth. States, especially great powers, *always* have alternative courses of action. The most a denial of choice can mean is that in a particular context, in pursuit of an inflexible goal, no alternative strategy seemed as desirable to the responsible policymaker. This translation of the phrase to read, "we had no alternative *that the Establishment would accept,*" is a far different and much less mechanistic formula.

This general point is a way of denying in advance the claim that the United States "has no choice" but to oppose de Gaulle and maintain its position on NATO integration, the approach to the Soviet Union, economic integration, and the American leadership role. Faced with the situation in the Atlantic world, the United States has several choices open to it, from which it must ultimately choose. Students of strategy have long known that failure to choose is itself a choice; equally relevant, however, is whether or not the refusal to decide is deliberate (that is, an acceptance of the status quo) or inadvertant (because the policy-makers failed to appreciate that alternatives were open and decisions necessary). It is possible—perhaps it is even defensible—for the United States to continue to follow the line in Europe that it has taken since 1961. But this is not the *only* possible course, nor necessarily the best.

At least four different alternative lines of policy are open to the United States today. We are speaking here of basic concepts, not elaborate implementation, and in the realm of action perhaps the several courses overlap. In concept, however, each incorporates a distinct vision of European-American relations.

The first alternative is of the "let's keep doing what we're doing" genre. Basic U.S. policy is to cling to the Atlantic formulas of 1949 in the face of all objections, to press harder for implementation of these doctrines, to give no ground in the face of resistance, and to be confident that history will prove the correctness of the American position. This course of action has several important virtues. First, it is not only familiar but established; all important decisions that went into it were made years ago, and the only problems involved in its prosecution now are administrative. Second, it is accepted—if not completely understood—by the American body politic. The public has become accustomed to the symbols of the Atlantic alliance, to NATO and the EEC, and even to such esoteric concepts as "integrated command." Officials can count on an active consensus in support of their moves. Third, the institutional structure, both domestic and international, for this policy already exists.

This policy of the status quo is admittedly treated lightly here but has been well elaborated earlier—and in literally hundreds of other books, articles, and speeches during the past five years. What can be said against it? Why have we argued that its present status and future prospects are so dim that it should be abandoned now?

We have answered the major parts of these questions many times already: the policy no longer fits the European reality or the interests of any of the participants except the United States. Still, Americans apparently reason that—in a thought borrowed from the communists—"time is on our side" in Atlantic relations. The American response to dissent in Europe today, as it has been since 1951, is one of patiently repeating the formulas, tolerating moderate disagreement, and applying direct pressure on any ally that shows signs of potentially dangerous "deviationism."

But there is no reason for any American to feel confident that "time is on our side" in European relations. It is true that General de Gaulle is an old man and that he will some day cease to be President of France. Some Americans undoubtedly feel that his disappearance will immediately restore the "good old days"; but the good old days never existed outside the imagination of American ideologues. To imagine that de Gaulle's name will turn out to have been "writ in water," and that his disappearance will automatically eliminate the ideas he has advocated since 1958, is to indulge in dangerous self-deception.

Existing American policy does not work now and promises to cause greater and greater trouble in the future. Indeed, it is probably the least workable of the four alternatives we are canvassing here.

The second alternative approach for the United States involves at least tacit acceptance of some of the European facts of life. It would abandon the notions of Atlantic "community" or a united Europe under American leadership; instead, the alliance would include only those states that accept the controlling American formulas of the past two decades—however few that might be.

This idea of a "smaller but tighter" alliance won some support in official American circles during the 1966 NATO crisis. To counter General de Gaulle's demand that foreign forces and NATO headquarters quit France, Washington began to speak openly of a NATO without France to be dominated by an American-British-German directorate.

This tactic has the advantage of preserving the military structure of the alliance at the cost of reducing its political viability. The major question it leaves unanswered, of course, is what to do about the defense of those ex-allies who have left the organization? Are they to be awarded to the Soviet Union as some form of international political door prize, or are they to be defended by American nuclear power anyhow? If the latter, what is the advantage of preserving NATO's formal military structure if recalcitrant, has-been allies can profit from the alliance on the same terms as full members?

Obviously, this alternative would allow the United States to adapt to major European changes without the embarrassing need for new concepts or policies. U.S. principles (1949 vintage) would, at least in theory, remain unimpaired; only their area of application would change. Nor should we overlook the possibility implicit in what American sources were calling, in the summer of 1966, the policy of the "empty chair." The theory behind that approach is that France has only temporarily absented itself from the alliance, forcing the remaining members to readjust their relations to take account of the vacancy. But France's chair would always remain at the council table, and Paris would be welcome to take up its old role anytime it wished. Thus, the second alternative would slide imperceptibly into the first, and the United States would be safely in the bosom of the status quo.

The major failure of this alternative is its lack of realism. A "NATO without France" is no NATO at all; a German-British-American triumverate would not be acceptable to the other members of the alliance for long. The United States has not won much support in its attempt to read France out of the alliance, nor is there reason to believe that France's withdrawal would result in a tighter and more binding set of understandings among the remaining fourteen members. The opposite case is more likely: in an alliance dominated by a three-power directorate, including Germany, the other members would probably try to reduce and blur their obligations to the group.

The third viable policy alternative for the United States involves a complete conceptual break with the past, the abandonment of the entire notion of an Atlantic alliance, the reduction of American political and military commitments in Europe to bilateral arrangements with one or two strong and politically reliable allies (Britain and Germany), and the acceptance of a completely free-wheeling great-power role for the United States. It demands an entirely new outlook on the world and America's role in its affairs. Put in such blunt terms, its ingredients may sound startling —even shocking—to Americans who have grown accustomed to the rhetoric of alliance. Yet such a course of action is no less than what France and certain other European states have accused the United States of following under the cloak of Western solidarity—and no less also than what great powers have always done in the past.

Note that this approach calls for the open disavowal of the entire ideological-intellectual apparatus on which the United States has relied for two decades in shaping its European policy—Atlantic solidarity, European unity, integrity of the free world, and all the rest. Such wholesale junking of well-worn and familiar concepts is of course out of the question as long as the United States remains true to its twenty-year image of the Cold War as the single orienting factor of national mission. But Americans do not realize that so much of their easy commitment to the European-American alliance is grounded on a particularly militant view of Soviet-American relations. Let the psychology of détente win mass acceptance in America, and many unacceptable (or even inconceivable) ideas will gain dramatically in attractiveness.

Leading and maintaining a large and cumbersome alliance, for example, might come to look more and more like a burden in a post–Cold War atmosphere. Direct great-power contacts and the prospect of concrete results might seem much more promising than the querulous leadership of a fractious group of smaller associates. Freedom of maneuver and unilateral decision are important to major states, perhaps more important in the end than extensive networks of commitments that seem to cost more than they are worth.

All of which is to say that only a reorientation of Cold War attitudes by Americans is necessary to make this third alternative minimally acceptable as a basis for action. But we are a long way from this moment; there is no prospect for the kind of breakthrough in Soviet-American relations that would cause the United States to abandon its standard world outlook. Whenever the reassessment actually takes place, this approach will become immediately relevant.

We must keep in mind that this is essentially a policy of negation and withdrawal, of reduction of commitments, and a rethinking of the bonds of alliance. Such a policy is always easier than a positive one of developing new linkages, objectives, and strategies. The United States could activate this alternative with only a few overt moves, almost without preparation or warning, at the moment it became disillusioned with its European venture and convinced that great-power relations would be more rewarding than a decaying alliance. Americans should always keep in mind the possibility of such a sudden reversal; Europeans are not only aware of its existence but concerned lest it be translated into reality in a "typically American" burst of activity.

We come now to the fourth alternative, the one favored

and defended in this book: a partnership in European-American relations. This is a deliberate policy choice for Washington; merely wishing for a better climate or waiting for something to turn up for the better, is not likely to bring success, nor is it appropriate to the major role America wishes to play in world affairs.

Partnership is the preferred alternative for several simple and, it would appear, self-evident reasons. First, the other three approaches all contain more objections than advantages, and partnership becomes increasingly attractive as the only open choice with meaningful prospects for improved relations. Second, partnership provides a conceptual basis for the United States to develop and maintain close and enduring ties with all European states, regardless of the course of the Cold War. Third, partnership allows America to recapture the sense of initiative and movement that characterized its European policy during the late 1940's, but never since.

The essence of partnership is that the United States, in deciding and planning its Atlantic policy, accept the fact that it is no longer a free agent. It is so closely tied with its associates—to a considerable extent, due to its own actions —that its every move is or ought to be a joint one. There can be no fundamental differences of interest between Western Europe and America if the alliance is to survive at all. Policy-making must go forward within a different framework. Europeans must be brought into the planning process fully, unreservedly, and ungrudgingly from the beginning of each policy enterprise. They must be permitted to influence American action in a crisis as well as in a routine operation. What emerges in action must be a joint product which all can support.

What Americans seem to overlook in the contemporary debate is the simple fact that consensus is the only basis upon which non-coercive international relationships can be built. A revised and refurbished Atlantic alliance must be based firmly on the consensus that ties the two sides of the North Atlantic together today. There has been almost no disposition in the United States—and very little in Western Europe either—to investigate seriously the nature of the common interests that knit together the members of a future Atlantic community. It is high time some serious attention was paid to these and related problems.

So long as Europeans admit—even only in principle—that the West must guard against a Soviet threat, the United States retains both a bargaining position and a real posture in and toward Europe. The question is not, however, whether America "can stay in Europe," or for how long. Much more important, for the longer term, is whether American policy is taking advantage of the breathing space provided by the continuation of the threat to pursue actively new policy lines. Clearly it is not.

The need for a new, forward-looking approach has not been entirely ignored in Washington policy-making circles. But any new attack on the problem requires major modification in the status-and-role implications of Atlanticism, and to an important degree some dilution of U.S. "leadership." Brought to this point by relying on abstract and theoretical formulations, American policy-makers have recoiled from embarrassingly specific policy choices. Discussion of "partnership" in the United States government is seldom encouraging for advocates of change. For all its shortcomings, existing American policy always seems—to the State Department—preferable to any new attack.

The Concept of Partnership

What, then, is involved in "partnership"? What changes in outlook, in approach, and in image would be necessary for the United States to accept as a basis for its European policy the currently popular observation that "the age of leadership has ended, the age of partnership has begun"? Why is it so difficult to reach even the exploratory decisions looking toward a partnership?

In essence, partnership is founded upon a status relationship of *equality,* while leadership (as American dogma has interpreted it for two decades) rests upon a status relationship of *inequality* and *subordination.* These latter characteristics of American policy have proved the most unpalatable to newly sensitive Europeans; modifying them will go far to restore a working relationship.

Yet, say Americans, Europe aspires to equal status, while the facts of life are that Europe is not and can never be equal to the United States in military strength or potential energy. So long as Western Europe remains divided into small and medium-sized states, all of them potentially quarrelsome and prone to eccentric bursts of individuality, to discuss European-American relations in a context of equality is to delude oneself. Even a united Europe would be caught in an unequal and inferior position vis-à-vis the United States. American logic contends, therefore, that Europeans are wasting time in a digressive and inevitably fruitless search for something called equality. Instead they should be considering how best to organize themselves into a cooperative free-world effort firmly under American leadership.

Europeans generally point out that the essence of the

argument is much more subtle than the United States makes it out to be. They make no attempt to deny the military facts, but they contend that they are substantially beside the point. The equality Europeans seek is one of *status,* not of *role.* They want the United States to recognize that the ambitions, goals, and interests of any European member of the Atlantic alliance are intrinsically as worthy as those of the United States. Europeans call for abandonment of the American doctrine that America's purposes are everyone's purposes, and that disagreement with the United States is *prima facie* evidence of turpitude by a minor ally.

Equality of status is demonstrated by equality of deference, and here the problem becomes most difficult. For the United States to change its attitude toward its allies is in one sense the easiest and quickest reform; but practically such a reversal in outlook is one of the most difficult changes to bring about. It is no easy matter for a people who have grown accustomed to receiving more deference than they give in return suddenly to content themselves with parity.

The issue is complex as well. Like all upward-mobile individuals, groups, or classes, Europeans will never be satisfied with a forced and grudging concession of formal equality, for the suspicion will linger that Americans, convinced against their will, will remain "of the same opinion still." Thus—as has been evident in the civil rights struggle in the United States—one group demands a change of heart while the other attempts to get away with only superficial and token concessions. The deference issue in Atlantic relations today is at the bottom of the entire problem.

Partnership, in other words, demands at the very least an explicit rejection of stratification in the alliance. Yet Americans do not admit that they have in any sense relegated Europe or Europeans to an inferior role; the arrangements against which de Gaulle protests were not established to guarantee American hegemony but rather to provide the best (that is, the most efficient) method of common defense. Americans ask what greater proof of European equality could be offered than the American commitment to regard an attack on Europe as an attack on the United States.

Again the old frustration: the American argument is very persuasive to Americans—and may indeed be objectively correct. Yet Europeans are no longer satisfied with it, demanding instead some more positive and effective formula of equality. And such is the nature of alliances that as long as the United States wishes to keep the Atlantic community intact, Europe will set the effective terms of the arrangement.

Any concept, therefore, of European-American partnership must rest on developing those areas of interest that are common to the United States and the states of Europe. Generally speaking, these include Soviet-Western relations, European development, and settlement of the outstanding questions left unanswered by World War II. Seen in this way, partnership takes on a decidedly regional cast; it is not automatically extended (as Washington has been prone to do) to include a global role for the European partners. Rather, European-American partnership must rest firmly on an identity of specifically Atlantic interests; extraregional cooperation should proceed on an ad hoc basis (such as coordinated aid programs), and divergent interests and resultant policies should be respected as perfectly legitimate. Consultation must either be reciprocal or undertaken only in areas of common interest. This of course assumes and requires the establishment of inter-governmental groups whose job will be to study and if possible expand the items on the agenda of common extra-European interests.

Operationally, a partnership would incorporate a different kind of common mission. Voluntary consensus is the key to effective cooperation in any kind of interstate arrangement, and this is nowhere more true than in the establishment and pursuit of common goals. The partnership would incorporate only those objectives accepted by the consensus of the membership.

American criticism rejects this idea as a policy of "the least common denominator." The United States says it would take kindly neither to the painful task of winning support, country by country and politician by politician, for its proposals, nor to confining itself to inadequate measures simply because they were the only ones acceptable to the whole group. Yet, vexing as it may seem to militant American policy-makers, there is no real alternative: in the future —as it has neglected to do in the past—the United States must win free consent from its allies on an almost issue-by-issue basis. No longer will the U.S. be able to risk defying the European consensus or attempting to split it.

Nowhere is consensus more important than in questions of decision-making. No U.S. practice has caused more hard feeling in Europe nor done more to underscore the inferior status of European allies than Washington's preference for unilateral decisions on questions affecting all members—to which the entire alliance is expected to conform. Exhibit A in this connection, as we have seen, is the American strategy reversal from massive retaliation to flexible response in 1962, but there are many others.

The shibboleth of "consultation" has obscured much of the discussion of decision-making. The United States believes it meets the requirements of intra-allied consultation if it communicates its decision to its allies (at least to its important allies) before taking action; whenever possible, furthermore, this information is transmitted far enough in advance of action to permit some discussion within the alliance. But Washington does not feel obligated to consult in emergency situations (such as the Cuban missile crisis) or in situations governed by "objective facts" which render

discussion useless (such as adoption of flexible response).
Under these circumstances, Americans insist that efforts to
consult would only waste time and unnecessarily excite
emotions.

Washington may admit the desirability of consultation to
give the allies a "sense of participation" (to borrow a phrase
from the MLF debate), but it has never seen any connection between the consultative process and the ultimate decision. When the United States invites its associates to express their opinions on a question, it does so for reasons
of courtesy or curiosity, or to solicit support; it is not generally interested in any game of give-and-take. Even the
Jackson Committee found something to criticize in the
1962 flexible-response decision and admitted that com-
puter-spawned pronouncements created intra-alliance difficulties that have not yet been overcome, especially in relations with France, "whose President, like most chiefs of
state, does not accept short shrift easily."

Consultation, to be real, requires not only that projects
be discussed jointly in advance of action, but also that comments from allies be taken seriously and incorporated into
the final decision. There is a world of difference between
telling allies, "This is what we are going to do; are there
any questions?" and asking them, "What shall we do?"
Europeans insist that partnership necessitates effective consultation by all members and requires that joint policies be
determined by a genuinely collective process.

Early in 1966 the Jackson Committee offered its own
definition of partnership (without, however, giving it that
name): "What the allies, including West Germany, need is
confidence that they are, in fact, involved in major issues of
strategic and political planning in such ways as *to influence
the actions of the United States government* in a crisis" (p.
12, italics added). Partnership requires that European
members of the alliance develop, maintain, and employ the

capacity to affect American decisions; but the preponderance of U.S. nuclear capability makes it certain that the reverse will always be true. Europe's disenchantment with NATO as it has evolved—and therefore with the whole Atlantic relationship—has grown from its inability to influence American decisions while remaining vulnerable to their effects.

It is more important now for the United States to make concessions to Europe's sensibilities in verbal and nonspecific terms than to establish a complete mechanism of consultation and joint decision. But American policy always shies away from agreements "in principle," preferring to pin down every detail before announcing any kind of agreement. It has not gone unnoticed in European circles that this traditional American approach is a useful tactic in the hands of a government that is not interested in reaching agreement at all, and Americans have been accused of bad faith in rejecting the principle in favor of tedious arguments about structure. Again, however, the trend of the times is in the opposite direction, and the acceptance of a principle with no binding arrangements may be easier for the United States in the future.

If the scope and method of a partnership are consensually determined, then another ingredient of the new arrangement must be faced. Probably an Atlantic partnership would pursue a much more limited role than NATO did at the height of its acceptance—and, as a matter of fact, than it does today. If French hints at the reconstruction of NATO are at all indicative of European thinking on the subject, a partnership would be much simpler organizationally and probably would interfere much less with the independent foreign policies of its members.

Such truncation of the alliance's scope and competence is clearly contrary to U.S. interests, as long as America hopes to retain its dominant role in the alliance. But, were partnership to replace leadership, and were it made explicit that all obligations were reciprocal, the United States would be in the same predicament as the other members and would find a reduction in the alliance's pretensions much more acceptable.

Most of the Atlantic argument, as presented in Washington, has rested on the valid point that Western Europe is still completely dependent on American nuclear guarantees for its security. The day is still far in the future when Europe will have sufficient strategic nuclear capability to deter effectively Soviet military might. But what the United States seems officially to have forgotten is that an America deserted by Europe would be in dangerous and painful isolation. Partnership should not be conceived of as a means of perpetuating Washington's "leadership of the free world" but as a way to increase jointly the ability of Europe and America to deal effectively with identifiable common problems. Admittedly, these concerns will be more limited in scope than those originally assumed by the United States after World War II. But the difference is that they will be dealt with effectively. Washington must decide between realistic achievements and improbable possibilities.

We have been emphasizing that partnership is a political concept, whereas leadership—as interpreted by America for twenty years—is apolitical and heavily military. The European revolt against NATO, and especially France's forceful language, has been more than anything else an attempt to pull the alliance dialogue back from its obsessive but irrelevant considerations of military technicalities to the real stuff of Atlantic relations: the political dynamics of the Atlantic nations. Washington has resisted this trend stubbornly; the Jackson Committee report—that invaluable compendium of Establishment arguments—put it this way (both tipping America's hand with reference to China and disposing of the French demand to discuss political arrangements):

> If the threat to the allies changes or if their interests would be served by a change in the scope of NATO's concerns—if, for example, Communist China proves in due course to be the principal threat to their survival in freedom or if economic, social, and cultural developments make closer political links between the allies desirable—the time will come when the allies may wish to re-form NATO to meet the new challenges and opportunities.
>
> But at the moment the urgent task is to put the interallied dialogue on a practical footing—to cope with the hard issues of the present. . . ." (p. 13)

These "hard issues of the present" include, of course, the standard catalog of American concerns. We search in vain for any admission that the political underpinning of the alliance requires scrutiny; indeed, the only reference to NATO as a "political arrangement" concerns the extent to which "the facts of power impose a special responsibility for leadership" on the United States.

But some second thoughts have been entertained in high American circles. When the Senate Foreign Relations Committee opened its hearings on Atlantic relations in 1966, there was a refreshing willingness on the part of the witnesses (including several long identified with NATO affairs) to admit that "political imagination," rather than what the Jackson Committee had called "managerial pseudo-science," was demanded from the United States if the alliance was to be preserved in any form acceptable to the American government and public.

We may sum up this general discussion of partnership by one final quotation from the Jackson Committee report:

All agree, President de Gaulle included, that the alliance has unfinished business. Its record since 1949 is one in which all can rightly take pride. But alliances are mortal. Like old generals, they may simply fade away unless they are used by, and useful to, national governments in dealing with their real, pressing problems. (pp. 13–14)

Indeed, NATO has been fading away in recent years, and this is the reason for the crisis in Atlantic relations. This quotation correctly diagnoses the cause of the decline as well: NATO is no longer considered useful to the national governments in "dealing with their real, pressing problems." An alliance with a heavily military outlook, an elaborate organization, and a strong leadership has lost its relevance to Europeans; only a political partnership with America can fill the void.

Europe as Partner

The practical requirements for partnership involve those factors that impose inequality and subordination on Europe today. As we analyzed them earlier, they are three: Europe's military weakness, lack of unity, and instability and immaturity in making policy in a complex world. Accepting Europe as a partner will force Americans to modify their attitudes toward each of these, not so much in terms of denying their existence (at least the first two are simple and obvious facts) but rather by reevaluating their policy relevance.

We have already indicated at several points how the fact of Europe's military weakness has lost significance to the extent that the common problem is no longer exclusively or primarily military in nature. Conversely, the United

States continues to insist upon the centrality of military security considerations, because in this realm American preponderance is beyond question.

Partnership, however, is a political and not a military concept. In a partnership grounded on equality of status and legitimate national interests, considerations of military inequality would be of minor import and relatively simple to resolve. The great American dream—specialization of roles and missions in the common defense—might even become a reality if a new, more meaningful, and universally accepted common mission, based on inter-allied consensus, governed the decisions of the membership.

Likewise, were the United States to quit seizing on every disagreement in Europe as proof that "Europe needs America," and were it instead to accept the phenomenon of "Europe uniting" as a basis for planning and decision, a very different climate for policy-making would prevail. Of course, such a suggestion would immediately run afoul of a chorus of protests from the "realists" in Foggy Bottom: there is too much risk in this approach; the Soviet Union would immediately take advantage of any leeway to split the West, and so on and on.

Even those in the American Establishment who have subscribed to European political and economic integration tend to identify too strongly with the federative theory, and so they collide with the confederationists-functionalists-nationalists led by France. Even occasional American support of unity has deepened the division rather than helped to heal it.

Would it not be a welcome change in American policy, as well as a most positive innovation, for the United States to adopt a course that contributed most directly to the future effective unification of all Western Europe? Can apologists for U.S. policy honestly claim that during the past six or seven years Washington has consistently sought maximum speed and maximum scope for the movement toward unification, or can they claim that official policy has never discerned any clash between European unity and "an Atlantic community"—under American leadership? A frank avowal by Washington that a tightly unified Europe is in the long-range interest of the United States, and that in the meantime America will not seek short-term profit from the ebb and flow of intra-European politics, would surely have a salutary effect on relations.

In the meantime, however, Europe remains divided. France (or West Germany, or Britain) has no right to speak for "Europe"—but each of these nations speaks quite clearly and unequivocally for itself. Lacking the opportunity to welcome a united Europe as the partner of the United States, Americans must somehow make the massive effort to consider each individual European country as the equal of the United States. Nothing more difficult can be imagined—yet nothing is more essential to avoid the collapse of the Atlantic alliance.

Here we come to the third point: Europe's "instability" and "immaturity" in policy-making. Logic and argument are of no use at this juncture, if Americans cannot see the political capability and wisdom of the various European leaders. If one adopts the working definition of "immaturity" as any behavior that contradicts U.S. policy, then Americans can continue to persuade each other that Europeans cannot be trusted to make their own policy. It is a comforting thought, particularly to one who finds reality in the organizational pyramid of such an entity as NATO.

But what logic cannot accomplish is being brought about by experience. Americans are discovering that Europeans are going right ahead and making their own decisions regardless of what the United States thinks about them. Washington may disagree, scold, threaten, or attempt to retaliate—the process continues unabated. Rightly or wrongly,

Europeans prefer to be the principal custodian of their important interests rather than to confide them to the United States.

So it serves no useful purpose for Americans any longer to deny Europe's competence in policy-making, for Europeans are making policy every day. It is much more necessary that the U.S. recognize this situation and the overwhelming probability that Europe will go on indefinitely making its own decisions—that this is the "new normality" of Atlantic relations. American policy can then get down to the important matters of translating partnership from abstract theory to concrete practice.

Chapter Eight
A New Policy:
Partnership
in Practice

Let us assume for the sake of argument that the United
States has accepted "partnership" as the new basis for its
European policy. Washington's change of heart is not a
gimmick designed to get concessions from Europeans; nor
is it a tactical maneuver for short-run gains, to be abandoned as soon as the situation "improves." No, American
policy sees partnership as the optimal European-American
relationship.

What policy consequences now follow? Here the transition from theory to practice, from partnership as concept
and image to partnership as a guide to decision-making in
the real world, becomes frightfully difficult. At this point
unofficial and non-Establishment critiques of American policy often go badly astray; factual ignorance and operational naiveté often turn well-intentioned polemics into un-

197

conscious farce. It is a danger which has silenced many promising voices.

Yet, if the notion of partnership described in the preceding chapter has any validity at all, it ought to have enough strength to lay the basis for some general observations about concrete policy for America. Certainly it should suggest new emphases, new purposes, and new criteria of success to replace those that have grown slippery and imprecise with use.

European-American partnership, as we have indicated, must rest on and develop from the elusive (and often abused) idea of "interdependence." When President Kennedy first elaborated it, interdependence was a dynamic and challenging concept around which Atlantic relations could be rebuilt. Now, through misuse and endless argumentation, it has become trite and virtually meaningless. What, then, should it mean in Atlantic relations?

Atlantic interdependence implies a mutually beneficial relationship among the states of the North Atlantic region. It does not describe objective realities as much as it indicates worthwhile possibilities. It does not assume the existence of an indivisible Atlantic Community of interest, but it does point the way to realistic achievements through coordination. It *requires* nothing but *inspires* much.

The fruits of interdependent Atlantic relationships are generally interpreted parochially on both sides of the ocean: Europeans see only the adjustments the United States ought to make; America sees only the concessions Europe must make. Both miss the main point: interdependent partnership, resting as it must on regional consensus, requires reassessments and adjustments on both sides, by all parties, in the interest of identifiable common interests.

Political Partnership

Certainly it is self-evident that partnership is a political concept and draws its vigor from harmonization of the political purposes of all the partners. Earlier we stressed the consensual element in decision-making. Thus the practical conclusion is that for the United States to adopt partnership, it must begin by realistically harmonizing its purposes with those of its allies.

To generalize broadly, Europeans have two major political concerns today. First, they are vitally interested in bringing the Cold War between the Soviet Union and the United States to a close, at least in so far as it affects them; this takes the form of constant agitation for further progress toward some formula of détente. Second, they are consumed with the problems of their own future: the shape of the new Europe and its role in the world. Obviously, these two concerns interact, for Europe can discover its long-term role only in a climate of stability and peace.

In these terms Europe seeks a working partnership with the United States. Europeans hope that the United States will continue to lead them but in a dramatically different direction. They want equality in decision-making on matters relating to East-West relations—but under the protective umbrella of U.S. power.

Once the blight of the Cold War is lifted from Europe, Europeans expect effective and rational cooperation with America in practical political enterprises. These would include not only the fulfillment of European aspirations toward unity but also such important issues as the long-term nature of European-American relations (what, after all, is involved in the Atlantic bond after the Soviet threat is removed?) and Europe's world role. In many ways these longer-range concerns are more difficult to resolve than the immediate problems of the Cold War, and yet they carry much more potential significance.

Americans must decide to what extent they are willing to identify themselves with European aspirations, for it is in these terms that the price of partnership must be paid. Dealing with a vitalized and dynamic Europe on a basis of status equality naturally demands a scaling back of American pretensions. How far will the United States be willing to go?

One would have to be blind to the history of the past two decades to deny that the Cold War has been very useful to American policy in many parts of the world—not the least in Europe. With the Soviet menace providing a built-in rationale and direction for most policy decisions, and with the organized free world conferring prizes of status and decision-making on the United States, Americans have grown attached to the institutionalized and more or less stabilized struggle with the Soviet Union. Yet today it has become a wasting asset: Cold War rhetoric no longer moves Europe, and maintaining the necessary hostility becomes increasingly costly. Americans are beginning to contemplate the world "after the Cold War" with more realism and considerably less panic than a few years ago.

As a result, the only basis for European-American ties is partnership founded on a set of common purposes transcending the Cold War; and it is of major importance that the United States decide for itself how intimate the partnership should be. It is not necessarily true that the closer the tie, the better for everyone; there will certainly be post–Cold War situations in which American and European interests might conflict. To be specific: how far should the United States go in supporting the two major European concerns we identified above—ending the Cold War and plotting the European future?

Certainly the first—a search for détente—is as much in the interest of the United States as of Europe. None of the long-range American goals for Europe can be achieved in a climate of East-West hostility; even the most sacred of clichés, the reunification of Germany, can become reality only through reasonable negotiation with Moscow and never by *force majeure*. NATO—the epitome of Cold War rigidity—has done all it can. The next step calls for flexibility and maneuver rather than confrontation.

The logic is unanswerable that the United States has the power to revitalize the alliance and restore much of the previous glamour to its leadership role in Europe. All it need do is develop (in full and honest consultation) with its allies a set of bargaining points to be used with the Soviet Union in the name of a united West. Whether or not negotiations actually produce détente is largely immaterial as far as the Atlantic alliance is concerned; much more important is that movement and progress would replace immobility as the guiding principle of the group.

In this connection, there are no longer any European takers for the American idea of the indivisibility of the struggle with communism. With American involvements with Chinese (or Soviet) power in non-European areas, the states of Europe have little concern and almost no interest. It will be enough for them to have their own bailiwick liberated from the Cold War, and they will take their chances elsewhere.

But what of the long-range interests held in common between the United States and an integrated Europe? How far should America go in sponsoring and assisting the return of European power and influence to a central place in world affairs? Is there really any basis for permanent European-American cooperation?

Opinions will legitimately differ in both the United States and Europe as to how close the two partners should be in the post–Cold War future. We argue here an extreme position: it will be in the permanent interest of the United States to be as close to an integrated Europe as it can manage. Maximum European-American identity on all questions is impossible, but partnership should be intimate and close-knit on the range of subjects it chooses to include.

This implies that partnership should be reinforced initially with agreements (and common policies which will logically follow) in areas of greatest immediate concern. For example, problems dealing with the settlement of post–World War II questions fall into this category. In the spirit of political partnership—keeping in mind the dual primary concerns of the Europeans: détente and integration for growth—collective European-American proposals for negotiating with East European states and the Soviet Union should be drawn. After the euphoria and good will that can result from an agreement through partnership in these ripe areas, the partnership can move to harmonize and coordinate future policies in extra-European affairs. Problems involving global European-American concerns will not lend themselves easily to solution by the adoption of joint postures; but given a spirit of cooperation developed and a momentum gained by effective coordination in European questions, the likelihood for coordinated extra-European policies will increase by leaps and bounds. "Consultation," which means information exchange after the fact, and the constant bickering that follows, will be abandoned. In its place there will arise joint planning in a spirit of mutual benefit among all the partners. Granted that the U.S. would lose some of its freedom of action with respect to extra-European policies, but it would receive the positive support of its European partners, and its position overall would be strengthened.

In the post–Cold War atmosphere of world politics, great-power relations will be marked by flexibility and change in a constantly evolving environment. In terms of basic issues and probable orientation, Europe and America will be the closest of the major participants. They will have more in common and fewer important disagreements than any other pair of powers. It will be a priceless advantage for the United States to be able to count on effective cooperation from a powerful and resourceful Europe in a broad range of areas.

The United States should be willing to pay a rather high price for this important working relationship. Deference equality, as we know, is one coin in which the price must be paid, but there are others. In its realm of policy the United States must be prepared to modify and limit a number of its own economic, military, and political interests to make room for competing yet complementary European efforts. In Latin America, in Southeast Asia, in Africa, and in the Middle East, American policies will probably be transmuted into a common effort with Europe, with a corresponding diminution in America's ability to shape and control events.

Political partnership, in a word, means a new European-American relationship. In many ways the achievement of this new era will demand what might seem to be unreasonable sacrifices from the United States, most obviously in the so-called "right" of unilateral decision in the name of the group. Yet we have demonstrated again and again that any realistic alternative to partnership will cost more and produce fewer and less desirable results.

Military Partnership

Although the crisis in European-American relations today is most frequently phrased in military terms—at least in the United States—we have argued that military emphases in

American policy contribute to the crisis itself. The real issues in European-American relations do not cluster about questions of nuclear weaponry or integration of command, although American analysts love to prate about a "hardware" solution to the problem. Political issues are primary to Europe, and military questions can be solved only after the more pressing political difficulties have been removed.

But to downgrade military concerns is not to remove them. The Atlantic alliance has a military component, and American policy must adopt a satisfactory approach toward the fundamental (that is, the politically relevant) military questions before partnership can be viable.

Obviously, NATO, as originally conceived, as presently functioning, and as defended by the United States can never be an instrument of relationship among partners. In concept and operation NATO reflects a peculiar relationship, founded upon a particular strategic situation and committed to a narrow range of action.

Nor can NATO be "reformed." Here American doctrine is correct—a reformed NATO, with its fundamental concepts modified, would no longer be NATO. The alternative facing the United States is to cling to a shell of existing structures or to cut loose and seek some entirely new and different formula for military cooperation.

But there really is no choice. *NATO-à-l'américain* is disintegrating, and the United States can no longer avoid a hard reassessment of its military requirements in Europe. The syndrome, like measles, turns out to be self-limiting, and Americans will outgrow NATO as their European allies are doing.

If a new attack on military questions is in order, a more rational procedure would be one of priorities. If only parts of the existing military relationship can be preserved in the face of political change—the assumption on which this analysis rests—then what parts ought to be retained? Up to now the American position has been that preserving NATO's organizational structure will preserve the essential dynamic of the alliance. This cart-before-the-horse emphasis has proved its own futility.

Realistic American requirements and prospects for European-American military alliance can be arranged in the following order of priorities:

First: Continued American-European collaboration for the defense of Western and Central Europe against Soviet attack.

Second: Maintenance of a United States nuclear guarantee for Western Europe and its continued acceptance by the several European states.

Third: Continued American presence in Europe in the form of ground forces.

Fourth: Agreements governing the way the armed forces of the allies would be used in case of actual combat.

Fifth: Command, staff, and operational arrangements for the conduct of hostilities.

Conspicuously absent from this list, of course, is the integration of military command in peacetime, or the establishment of permanent structures for coalition policy. In these terms the partnership approach to military problems departs most sharply from existing American policy. How far the United States can proceed down the list of priorities depends upon the European threshold of acceptability rather than the persistence or skill of American negotiators. As in the political realm, the Europeans will decide how closely to the United States they will formalize their military destiny. There is not very much the United States government can do about it.

So-called "hardware" solutions to the dilemma of NATO, which seek to undermine political cleavages by various devices calling for the transfer—apparent or real—of nuclear weapons to some form of European control, are self-defeat-ing. Too many hard feelings have been engendered, too many unilateral decisions made, and too many slippery gimmicks attempted to trick Europeans into continued subordination, for a non-political overhaul of NATO to have a salutary effect.

Yet when Americans and Europeans agree on political goals and the costs of achieving them, all operational questions—including military ones—solve themselves easily and relatively painlessly. Partnership in military terms is impossible without a basis of political understanding.

So the most useful way for the United States to attack the thorny problem of nuclear weapons in NATO is to ignore it, or at least to minimize its technical aspects in favor of dealing with the political tension that has given it birth. An alliance founded upon a political partnership vitiates all the nasty questions about who owns, who commands, and who is responsible for national nuclear armories. For partners persuaded of the validity of their common mission, questions of command and ownership of nuclear weapons would assume an appropriately secondary role.

Arguments such as these, however, have difficult sledding in the United States today. In the name of "non-proliferation," American policy still opposes national nuclear deterrents in other hands—or insists upon unified (that is, American) command of all nuclear forces in the alliance. What underlies American concern over the French *force de frappe* is a political judgment that France might use its power for purposes which the United States disapproves, while de Gaulle has repeatedly explained that France's pursuit of national nuclear power is based on a lack of trust in America's political steadfastness. But American spokesmen still find it difficult to articulate political considerations, preferring to pretend that all political questions were answered years ago and that allied "commitment" to a 1949 model of NATO is irrevocably and forever fixed.

Economic Partnership

Economic partnership is perhaps the least difficult of the several varieties to implement but is also beset by political preoccupations. The United States and Europe are natural economic associates—developed countries are usually each other's best customers—and it would require only a few political decisions to make economic partnership a reality.

Back in 1962 the Kennedy administration made a brave start with its idea of an "Atlantic [trading] community," even though the concept was partly vitiated by the assumption that the community would be safely under American leadership. That America and Europe belonged together, and that their combined economic power would make an enormous difference to the rest of the world, was self-evident to the New Frontier.

President Kennedy's "grand design" came to grief with the failure of Britain to gain entry to the Common Market, and thereafter very little was heard about any concept of "community" in economic relations with Europe. The Kennedy Round of GATT negotiations limped along with economic nationalism the guiding principle on both sides of the Atlantic; by the end of 1966 hopes for any real progress had all but evaporated.

By the mid-1960's American economic power had surpassed that of the EEC and EFTA states combined and gave promise of widening the gap still more. This growth disparity gave rise to sincere European fears about "colonization" of European economies by American firms, perhaps even eventual takeover. Perhaps the most useful consequence of economic partnership would be a fresh and good-tempered attack on the problems of American economic penetration of Europe.

Here magnanimity and a refusal of American business to extract the last penny of profit from Europe would bring major political and economic returns. Americans may deride or ignore European fears of economic conquest, but the fears are real even if the danger is not, and they play their part in intensifying the general climate of crisis. Economic partnership must begin with elimination of European fears of American economic domination. With that issue settled, the way would be cleared for a direct attempt to create the trading partnership that, at least in theoretical terms, seems attractive to both sides.

Two preconditions must be met, however, before the Kennedy grand design may be used as a blueprint for partnership: the EEC must accept Britain (and, therefore, most of the other states of EFTA), and the United States must abandon its cherished dream of "leadership" over the greater trading community. The second would be a unilateral American decision. The first calls for the application of considerable diplomatic finesse and direct influence upon the decision-making machinery of half a dozen European states. Yet both are intrinsic to the larger concept of partnership, for implementation of *political* partnership by the United States would simultaneously reduce European (especially French) objections to British membership in the EEC and make membership much more attractive to London.

The trading community foreseen in 1962 is so central to the new partnership that it is worth a high price. It may well require junking some of the cherished elements of American protectionism and throwing the American market open to European imports on a hitherto unparalleled scale. This will mean some losses, and perhaps major sacrifices in some parts of the American economy. Yet the United States has no right to ask more of its trading partners than reciprocity.

Sacrifice and loss, however, are not the keys to the trading community; gain and profit are its inspirations. Loss on both sides will be temporary and localized, but profits will be permanent and general. It is a basic tenet of American free enterprise that competition means better service to the consumer as quality goes up and prices remain as low as possible. If Americans really believe this as it applies within the domestic market, they should welcome the opportunity to try it on a multi-national scale. The larger the scope of the free market, the greater the returns.

Economic partnership, likewise, will make possible a realistic and effective attack on the problem of development assistance to the emerging nations. The Organization for Economic Cooperation and Development, created at American insistence to spread the burden of aid more widely among the industrialized states, has not worked especially well. The problems of bilateral versus organizational arrangements, plus political "strings" attached to aid programs, show clearly that another approach is needed. The overall program of economic assistance undertaken by Europe and America has not achieved anything like its potential effect; at the same time, the United States—making "foreign aid" a Cold War weapon—has carried a disproportionate share of the entire load. Some better arrangement is certainly possible—and obviously necessary.

In European relations, the United States should not expect that economic measures, such as those we have discussed here, will do what political wisdom and political courage can alone accomplish. Economic partnership can follow political partnership; it cannot precede it or replace it. Politics remains central to the entire issue.

The Special Problem of Germany

Only two members of NATO have common frontiers with the Soviet Union—Turkey and Norway. Germany, however, is on the front line of the East-West confrontation in quite another way: only Germans have a direct territorial stake in the outcome of the struggle, and only they of all the members of NATO have virtually no foreign policy except the prosecution of these Cold War issues vis-à-vis the Soviet Union. All the other allies have interests and policies which in some way transcend direct confrontation with the communist bloc. Only Germany is so completely a victim of the Cold War.

The United States, highly sensitive to West Germany's key role in any bipolar approach to the Cold War, has seen to it that German concerns and issues have been made essential parts of the "common mission" of the free world. As we have noted, the United States has sought to perpetuate an image of steadfastness and firmness in Europe through total inflexibility on all German questions and by encouraging the Bonn government to do the same.

As a matter of fact, Washington has on many occasions seemed to be determined to be "more Catholic than the Pope" by going even further than responsible German officials in formulating a bill of particulars for German reunification. There is some evidence that West Germany has been embarrassed by the exigency with which Washington has pressed its claims—at least verbally. The vigorous manipulation of the symbols of German reunification and recovery have served to keep Soviet and East European fear and resentment alive and to reduce the likelihood of meaningful détente.

Just what effect will a European partnership have upon German-American relations and the special place that Bonn has occupied for so long as America's protégé? In a future that is full of difficult choices, none will cause more heartaches in Washington than the painful process of revising the German policy.

Modifying German policy is not merely a matter of modifying intra-allied relationships. Germany is in a front-line position in the Cold War, and any change in the texture or content of American commitments to, say, German reunification will be closely watched in the Kremlin. Coordinating such a dynamic and structural change in the alliance while simultaneously moving Soviet-American contacts from one plateau to another will be a massive challenge to American ingenuity and skill.

The twenty-year-old edifice of policy that the United States occupies (or hides behind) in Germany is a perfect illustration of the shortcomings we have argued against throughout this book. American defense of German reunification, German identification with the West, and liberation of Eastern Europe from Soviet domination are monuments to the doctrine that Soviet militancy can be dealt with best by constantly saying "No" and waiting for the Kremlin to change its mind. For at least fifteen years it has been evident that America's German policy was calculated to bring the Kremlin not to reason but only to obduracy. Reunification, NATO membership, EEC membership, and anti-communism formed a blueprint for Germany's future that Moscow could never accept. But Washington—with Bonn in its tow until very recently—has acted on the premise that half a loaf was worse than none as long as principles remained intact. Instead of gaining what it could for Germany out of the ebb and flow of Cold War relations, the United States has "stood firm" and achieved none of its stated goals for Germany.

So partnership with a uniting Europe implies détente with the Soviet Union and a major revision of American policy toward Germany. These two notions, as a matter of fact, go hand in hand; no meaningful security agreement with Moscow is possible without some major moves toward resolution of the German question. East-West agreement on Germany, reached in a climate of give and take, would force the United States to modify many of its long-standing claims. But its accomplishment is earnestly desired by all other members—including the bulk of German opinion—of the nascent partnership.

The German question may in fact be the hardest test of American sincerity in advocating real partnership. Very few of the other members of NATO, for example, share Washington's enthusiasm for German policy or are as confident that Germany has truly "reformed." Fears of a German-American "special relationship" at the core of the alliance have never been silenced since the United States first brought about German rearmament in the early 1950's. Washington's instinctive turn to Bonn to offset de Gaulle's militancy in 1966 did not go unnoticed in NATO capitals, and the reaction undoubtedly contributed to the lukewarm support America received.

So France especially and Europe generally will interpret the sincerity of America's quest for partnership by the yardstick of German policy. If the United States is willing to abandon its effort to vindicate Germany as the central aim of European policy, and if it instead directs itself toward larger European-wide concerns, then partnership can have a long-term meaning and force. As it seeks to recover a role in European affairs, the United States must persuade newly sensitive European attitudes that America takes Europe seriously on its own terms rather than as an incident in a global Cold War. The quickest way to the hearts and minds of contemporary Europeans is for the United States to relax its mechanical insistence on every semicolon and comma of its traditional formula for German settlement, and to articulate German affairs into an overall European-American consortium.

The question of Germany and its role in the Cold War has inspired American policy for the past two decades in Europe. In an era when change and a new approach are absolutely necessary alternatives to stultification and frustration, a new stance on the German question must be the first step toward a new European policy. Whatever the cost in intellectual distress and political embarrassment for the United States, the situation permits no lesser measures.

Toward Partnership: Some Recommendations

How, then, can the United States begin to salvage Atlantic relations? What should it do to begin working for an effective European-American partnership?

First, the United States must admit to itself and to its European allies that present difficulties result from fundamental misconceptions about the nature of the Atlantic alliance and the position of each of its members. Only by such a candid and fundamental admission will all the verbiage surrounding the present dialogue be flushed away. Once this is accepted, the invective and acrimony at debates over NATO structures and procedures will fade into irrelevance, and the real issues will come forward.

Second, the "real issues" of Atlantic relations and of European-American partnership must be defined. We have attempted merely to outline the main contours, for only silhouettes are now possible; but what more is called for?

Nothing short of immediate and broad action is needed. The Atlantic nations should establish a high-level study group of academic analysts and official policy-makers to define positive areas of mutual advantage. Our main concern here should be not with negative criticism of existing relations and institutions but rather with positive elaboration and innovation. We must try to indicate what can and should be done collectively, not what cannot be done individually.

Such joint analysis could not fail to be useful to all concerned. Instead of being content with vague formulations of a global holding operation, the Atlantic states would find themselves emphasizing creative innovation. The changed conditions in the region would be defined and their implications understood. Stale, ritualistic, and inflexible stances would be exposed as inappropriate, and the task of building a new relationship could begin.

In any sweeping reassessment and reorientation, the broad regional basis of partnership can be readily discerned. The states of Europe, the Soviet Union, and the United States are still the major participants in world affairs; within this grouping lies the overwhelming preponderance of power and influence—and the major sources of tension—in today's world.

It is becoming increasingly apparent that Europe, the Soviet Union, and the United States have a basic interest in strictly limiting their areas of conflict. Why couldn't this very interest be modified and expanded, directed into a regional settlement of outstanding interests? Prospects for détente, at least in Europe, have never been better; why not encourage their development? This is the major common interest between Europe and America today. From it flow many subsidiary areas of possible coordination. But it is central. This is why European-American partnership must be, initially, limited to the prime concerns of the Atlantic region.

The military aspects of partnership would allow simultaneous pursuit of at least four main objectives. First and foremost, the level of tension in Europe could be lowered further. Second, Western Europe could be encouraged to attempt continental military planning and coordination and would thereby experience immediate benefits and advantages arising from even imperfect coordination. Third, partnership would also insure the continued active presence and influence of the United States in Western Europe. Looked at in another way, Western Europe would be a massive and friendly buffer area separating the United States and the Soviet Union. Last, although not of least importance, an Atlantic partnership would effectively divide the responsibilities for containing communist power on a global scale. The objective of balancing the Soviets in Europe would be assumed by Europeans, freeing the United States to react more effectively to communist probes elsewhere in the world, should such probes manifest themselves.

The economic consequences and advantages of partnership have already been discussed at length. Suffice it to say here that both sides of the Atlantic dialogue realize the possibilities inherent in a massive trading community. What has not been investigated adequately is the probable dislocations and areas of potential conflict. The United States and Europe, if they are to seek actively the enormous economic benefits of partnership, must also be willing to make short-term sacrifices.

It is in the realm of economic partnership that the greatest possibilities for global coordination arise. Washington should propose and pursue a policy of aid coordination with Western Europe. An Atlantic aid organization (perhaps in cooperation with the United Nations), jointly administered by the member states, would go a long way toward reducing present conflicting aid programs to the developing nations. Developmental and technical assistance, without the political conditions Washington likes to attach to foreign aid, would thereby become more effective in its economic impact and far less costly to the donor states.

Political partnership means coordination and consensus. It applies first of all to settlement of East-West problems in Europe, détente with the Soviet Union, and reintegration of the two halves of the continent. But it also carries implications for other areas of the world. In concerns that are outside the immediate range of common regional interest, partnership means acceptance of controlled divergences. This requires admission of legitimate differences, but, more important, readiness to ameliorate them through compromise.

In the last analysis and within the bounds of realism, one must admit that a number of issues and policies will remain beyond coordination if the vital interests of the partners are too divergent. In this case, partnership would give way to peaceful competition. But such competition should never be so fierce as to affect coordinated and mutually beneficial policies elsewhere.

If America's goal is not to perpetuate its temporary leadership of a hastily conceived defensive coalition of nations, but rather to ensure the development of a stable world of peaceful change, then the concept of European-American partnership is admirably suited to the task. It alone offers prospects of success. But if the United States sacrifices long-range goals to misconceived short-term advantages, it must also reconcile itself to ultimate failure and loss of both. Achievement of a true European-American partnership founded upon a firm political understanding is so important to the United States that even at a high price it will be an attractive bargain. In no other way can the United States avoid another last chance in Europe.

Index

217